LIFE LESSONS OF A DESPERATE HOUSEWIFE

Kathryn Hendershot
With John Hendershot

Life Lessons of a Desperate Housewife by Kathryn Hendershot
Published by ANGELITA PUBLICATIONS
P. O. Box 411
Nicholasville, KY 40340

"Humpty Dumpty" from *The Christian Mother Goose Book* by Marjorie Ainsborough Decker, copyright 1977 Christian Mother Goose Book Company, Grand Junction, CO 81501. Used by permission.

All scripture quotations, unless otherwise indicated, are taken from the New King James Version®. Copyright © 1982 by Thomas Nelson, Inc. Used by permission. All rights reserved.

Scripture quotations taken from the Amplified® Bible, Copyright © 1954, 1958, 1962, 1964, 1965, 1987 by The Lockman Foundation. Used by permission. (www.Lockman.org).

Scripture quotations taken from the The Living Bible © 1971 by Tyndale House Publishers. Used by permission.

Scripture quotations taken from The Message © 1993, 1994, 1995, 1996, 2000, 2001, 2002. Used by permission of NavPress Publishing Group.

Scripture quotations taken from the New American Standard Bible®, Copyright © 1960, 1962, 1963, 1968, 1971, 1972, 1973, 1975, 1977, 1995 by The Lockman Foundation. Used by permission. (www.Lockman .org).

ISBN-10: 1-933858-21-4
ISBN-13: 978-1-933858-21-0
Library of Congress catalog card number: 2007926903

To those who are hurting and searching for meaning.
To those who are struggling through troubled relationships and feel isolated.
To those who are in need and overwhelmed with hopelessness.
And
To those who care about them.

CONTENTS

Acknowledgments   vii

Author's Note   viii

Preface   x

Part I: Seeking and Finding

  1. What's Real?   3

  2. My New Best Friend   9

  3. My Enemy Has A Name   13

  4. Yielding Control   17

  5. From Fantasy to Reality   21

  6. A Surprise Baptism   25

  7. What Am I Saying?   29

  8. Moving On   33

Part II: Humility and Forgiveness

9. Learning to Forgive 41

10. Facing the Reality of a Faulty Marriage 47

11. In the Midst of a Storm 53

12. Keep Holding On 59

13. A New Red Dress 67

14. Pressing In 71

15. A Clear Conscience 75

Part III: Healing and Walking

16. Healing Is Available 81

17. Stepping Out 91

18. My Hiding Place 99

19. Personal Care 105

20. God Has a Plan 111

Epilogue 117

ACKNOWLEDGMENTS

What a wonderful gift it is to have friends who share your trials as well as your joys. Suzanne and Ed Paxton have been such friends to John and I. When it came time for me to gather my final thoughts and direction, they graciously granted me a hide-away at "Our Point of View" (their home on Lake Cumberland). They later honored me by reading the manuscript and sharing their wisdom and editorial advice, which was greatly appreciated, as well as extremely helpful.

Eunice Irwin, another faithful friend, also came through with encouragement and practical help on this project. She generously provided the transportation necessary for the trip.

Thank you dear friends.

AUTHOR'S NOTE

The original version of *Life Lessons of a Desperate Housewife* was penned over twenty-five years ago, and is now out of print. This humble little effort to reach out to the lost, the struggling, and the hurting with a testimony of God's grace and goodness was received into thousands of homes and hearts throughout the years, even from as far away as Africa. Reports of God using it as a tool of ministry are still brought to our attention from time to time.

After sitting idly on my bookshelf for these many years, this little book came to my attention in the summer of 2005. I shared it with my daughter-in-law, and shortly thereafter a fellow doctoral student from Papua, New Guinea greeted me at the annual Fourth of July parade with, "Kathryn, I have just read your book." I thought he was speaking of my recently published dissertation that was fresh on the library shelves, but no. He continued, "I bought it at a yard sale!" I had a good laugh and thought nothing more of it until it was time to pack for a mission trip to Kenya.

I was going to be speaking to a women's group on the Book of Ruth, but I kept feeling drawn to the possibility of sharing my early testimony. Just before leaving for the plane I grabbed the little book off the shelf, and stuffed it into my carry-on. To my amazement I had forgotten many of the details of God's faithfulness.

Shortly after arriving in Kenya I was surprised with an invitation to speak at a Sunday morning service. I knew immediately that I would be sharing this testimony that was fresh on my heart once again. The Holy Spirit gently ministered to the hearts of the people that morning in very visible ways, and I remembered afresh how powerful our testimonies are—even those that took place long ago.

With this remembrance of what the Lord did and the obvious life that this testimony was still bringing forth, there came a calling to make it available once again. It is my earnest prayer that the Holy Spirit will minister new life to all those who ponder its pages.

PREFACE

"You are going to have a baby." These words flitted through my heart and soul for years. At first I took them literally, and expectantly waited for this miracle to be conceived. Gradually His message became clear—the Lord was calling me to be a channel of spiritual life.

In the spiritual realm, as in the physical realm, He is the Creator of life, but He allows His weak earthen vessels to share in the glorious life-giving process. My expectant heart is beholding this promise as I begin a labor of love. The seed was planted years ago when I entered into a personal relationship with Jesus Christ. A joyous new life began, and with it a driving desire to share His reality.

This desire has been nurtured and deftly directed through the years by the Holy Spirit. As an expectant mother in her last months of pregnancy becomes anxious and impatient, so have been my exhilarating expectations this past year. Just as she knows in the ninth month that the time is short, I too know that this blossoming within can no longer be constrained—it is the day of delivery!

PART I

SEEKING and FINDING

Chapter 1

WHAT'S REAL?

These words I speak to you are not incidental additions to your life, homeowner improvements to your standard of living. They are foundational words, words to build a life on. If you work these words into your life, you are like a smart carpenter who builds his house on solid rock. Rain poured down, the river flooded, a tornado hit—but nothing moved that house. It was fixed to the rock.

But if you just use my words in Bible studies and don't work them into your life, you are like a stupid carpenter who built his house on the sandy beach. When a storm rolled in and the waves came up, it collapsed like a house of cards.

Matthew 7:24 (The Message)

Reality has been an intangible, illusive commodity that has haunted my reasoning mind since early childhood. Echoing memories of questions such as, "Why are you here?" "Where did you come from?" "What happens after you die?" persistently pounded within my groping gray matter for over twenty years.

The vivid memory of an early childhood experience in questioning remains. "Where were you before you were born?" kept rolling around and around as if taped to a revolving door in my four-year-old mind. Clamping my chubby little hands over my ears, I pressed with all my might as if to push the questioning voice away, while screaming within, "No! No! No! I won't listen!" These questions were tormenting because their answers eluded me.

People today are running around as this four-year-old child with their hands clasped over their eyes and ears refusing to face the reality that we are here by God's creative design, that He made us, He loves us and He has a purpose for our lives individually and corporately—and our lives are intricately connected to Him.

Many have believed the lie that he or she who has the most toys, the sexiest image, and the highest IQ wins—refusing to listen to the truth that life is *not* all about us. Masses of humanity are insisting on living in a flimsy, empty illusion that somehow they are the center of the universe, while others are falling for the opposite side of the lie—that they are just a spec on this earth and therefore insignificant. All trying desperately to fill the emptiness, the *meaninglessness,* with things, work, status, entertainment, knowledge, fitness, sports, make-overs of various kinds, and/or relationships—but the "rat-race" speeds on, and the void is never filled.

I existed in such an illusion throughout my childhood and teens—constantly living in an "if only" world. "If only" the right guy would ask me for a date. "If only" I could drive. "If only" time would pass faster. "If only" I were prettier, smarter, and my parents wealthier. My mother would often comment that I was wishing my life away. When some of the "if onlys" were finally fulfilled their attractiveness instantly disintegrated into dust as the next "if only" billowed into a burst of alluring air.

September 4, 1965 was an enormously elaborate illusion day. It was wedding bells day. Our storybook romance and courtship culminated with all the traditional trimmings. Family and friends gathered in the appropriately cathedral-like "First" Church. The altar was skirted in white with breathtaking white bouquets symmetrically spaced behind it. The tall, thin candles stood at attention in the freestanding candelabras completing the vision of perfection and holiness.

My elegant peau de soi gown was a designer's original, and my beautiful bridesmaids donned Bonwit Teller's best. Each member of our wedding party could have been a professional model alertly posed as the minister pronounced us husband and wife.

REALITY: It *was* a lovely ceremony. It *was* a fun day. John and I were legally married. But we had known each other physically a couple months before the ceremony. We were not pure and holy. The guilt and frustration weighing upon me subtly stretched the vivid void within. Although we portrayed ourselves to be Christians (and thought we were), we were not. If anyone had asked us, we would have answered, "Yes, we are Christians." We had been to Sunday school and Church as we were growing up. We knew all about Jesus Christ—the Christmas story and the Easter story. But then, we knew all about Ronald Reagan too. We had seen President Reagan's pictures, and heard his speeches. We knew about his family, his ranch, and had even seen him in person—but we did not *know him personally*. We did not *know* Jesus Christ either.

Before the sun set that September Saturday, depression had begun to settle in as a deluge of disillusionment descended upon my heart. "Is this all there is?" The turbulent waters of loneliness that I thought marriage would still began to rise even more violently and drowned the remaining helpless hopes of "happily ever after."

The day after the wedding we traveled for eight sultry hours on the Pennsylvania Turnpike (no air conditioning in cars back then). When we got to our four-star hotel the bridal suite measured about a foot wider than the bed. Taking another disappointment in stride we decided things would look better after a nap, however, I awoke about an hour later to hear the muffled sobs of my knight-in-shining-armor. In startled unbelief I queried, "What's wrong? Are you sick?"

"No. Nothing's wrong" he moaned.

"Then why are you crying?"

"I don't know. I guess I'm just feeling the weight of my responsibility."

"What responsibility?"

"You. I'm responsible for feeding you, housing you, getting insurance to cover you..." his voice trailed off into a shouting silence.

Hurt, anger, and panic jockeyed for position and squeezed through the doorway of my emotions simultaneously. My combat technique was to pretend that nothing had happened and run!

Choosing to ignore John's agony, I mechanically dressed for dinner. We executed the maneuvers of dining and sightseeing and were relieved when those queasy waves of meaninglessness were once again swallowed up in sleep.

After a weary week on Cape Cod of simply trying to pass the time, we attempted to produce an award winning love scene by checking into a luxurious resort motel. But even this extravaganza fell through when John referred disapprovingly to my fitted black spaghetti-strap dress as a slip, and voiced his displeasure over the manner in which I ate my shrimp (with my fingers). The fragile breath of our immature love was being gradually, but steadily, snuffed out with each verbal blow.

Of course we returned home with glowing reports about the Cape. No one suspected how miserable it actually had been. We were so glad the fiasco was over that we were bubbling with joy, and everyone mistook our enthusiasm as an expression of marital bliss, instead of what it really was—the enormous relief of having survived the shock of our marital disappointment.

Once we settled into our apartment the rat-race routine soothed our strained relationship to a degree. We spent hours preoccupied with classes and studying, which served as a convenient camouflage for our lack of communication, but new bricks were continually being blasted into place upon the woeful walls that were rising between us.

Having grown up on Doris Day movies (the wife wearing a crisp little apron, with every hair in place and other unrealistic romanticisms), I would periodically inquire, "John, do you think I'm pretty?" He would invariably grunt, "Eh, you're okay." And all my dramatic dreams would go slithering down the drain.

The most powerful and protective value my parents instilled in me was that marriage is an "until death do you part" commitment. Before we were married, my mother told me that I could *never* come home because of an argument with John. Halfway out of Bowling Green, Ohio one Sunday afternoon her voice echoed in my ears. I obediently made a U-turn on Highway 6 and went back to John, determined to make it work.

We had fun times in those early years attending dances, plays, and ball games and we were sexually compatible. Our marriage *looked* good on the stage of life, but it *felt* unstable, cold and lonely. The daunting feelings were an undercurrent that we ignored. It is only in retrospect that we can face them realistically. We were building our marriage on a sandy beach.

Chapter 2

MY NEW BEST FRIEND

I am the way, the truth, and the life. No man comes to the Father except through Me.

John 14:6

Shortly after our first anniversary John proudly accepted a position with his family's heat-treating company. He began earning twice the salary he would have made had he finished another two years of college and taken a job teaching industrial arts. Circumstances were looking encouraging—surely a bulging bank account would provide the security I desperately sought.

That ominous autumn my mind drifted with the leaves, my emotions were more melancholy than usual, and my body languished under a variety of stresses. A problem with birth-control pills had caused severe hemorrhaging, and being an anemic basket case enhanced the feelings of meaninglessness. "Why am I here? What happens after you die?" Those old questions broke forth like an erupting vacuum. The fear of dying seesawed with a calm indifference.

John stood stoically beside my hospital bed looking like the fulfillment of my teenage dreams—tall and handsome in his new navy herringbone suit, but there was a dense distance between us, and he remained oblivious to the pulsating pain within me. After he left the room, God and I had a talk—life or death, it was up to Him. I did not care anymore.

We celebrated our second anniversary in the romantic Pocono Mountains. This was a definite improvement over our horrendous honeymoon. I was encouraged that God had restored me physically, and I felt a love for John whispering within my heart. We had endured much travail, and had hopes that our immature love was growing, and yet . . . .

Talking to God had always been a sacred corner of my life. Attending church and even endeavoring to read the Bible were sporadically resurrected goals. Therefore, when I became pregnant (after being told I would never be able to give birth) it was natural for me to diligently seek God's wisdom on how to be a good mother. I understood that biologically bearing a child would not automatically instill within me the attributes of motherhood. Although the answers were never obvious during the course of our one-sided conversations, my nagging fears were always calmed.

My whole world changed color the day that Kimberly Ann made her debut. Surely *this* was what life was all about. John seemed excited and my parents looked like a couple of glowworms! *Finally*, there was a purpose for living. Taking care of Kimberly was the most satisfying experience my heart had ever held. It was a pure, almost holy feeling having this little human being entrusted to my care.

On Kimberly's first birthday we had a lovely new home— swimming pool and all. John had a prosperous and challenging job, and we had a precious little girl. My list of "if only" was being fulfilled, but somehow my illusive bubble of happiness was still lisping.

That summer we were transferred to a little country town in South Carolina, where the atmosphere itself lured us to church. There is nothing like southern hospitality to soothe one's soul. Warm greetings were backed up with offers to help us get settled, and fresh produce from their gardens. And what a preacher! This handsome young man beamed a heartwarming smile, and his sparkling brown eyes were accentuated with a healthy bronzed tan. He simply introduced himself as Phil Jones. The love of God flowed through this man of the cloth, and we were impressed. Our antiquated image of the clergy was shattered—thank God!

But Phil was only a forerunner of the Man I was to meet the following Sunday. God was simply preparing my ears to hear, and my heart to receive what He had to say to me through His servant.

Phil began preaching about Jesus being a garbage man. Having been to church enough in my younger years to know the Christmas "story" and the Easter "story," I flinched when the words "garbage man" were spoken— they seemed sacrilegious. He continued, "Jesus came and collected all our garbage—our sin, and carried it to the cross with Him." I pictured Jesus in my mind— beaten, bruised, bleeding, and bent over with the weight of a huge bulging sack. This distorted baggage contained the sin of the world, and produced filthy rags out of His once pure white garment. Phil continued, "The Bible says that all of us are sinners and have fallen short of the glory of God simply because we have gone our own way, leaving God, our Creator, out of our daily lives." My mind flipped back to the Christmas story—Mary and Joseph in Bethlehem with no room at the inn for Jesus to be born. There had been no room in my inn, my heart, for Jesus to be born either. My spirit was hanging on to every word Phil uttered, as if it were life itself.

"God is a just God, and must punish sin. He is not the kindly grandfather type who looks the other way and excuses sin, but out of His great love for us He made a way to cleanse us from our sin—He sent His Son, Jesus, to be a garbage man for us. Jesus took the punishment for our sin, our garbage, when He died on the cross. He took your place on that cross. He shed His holy blood to cleanse us from our sin, and to save us from hell."

The truth Phil was preaching pierced my heart. For the first time in my life I understood why Jesus died on the cross. It was not because some men decided to crucify Him. He chose to lay down His life for me so that I would have a way to get to heaven. He had each of us, individually, on His mind when He suffered on that cross in our place.

Because of what He did, heaven is a free gift to us from Jesus. It is not something we can earn, or deserve because we are good. It is a gift we can receive by faith. This is not merely believing the facts in our head, nor is it the kind of positive thinking that gets you through an operation, but *saving faith* is trusting Jesus Christ *alone* for eternal life.

After the service I dropped on my knees in total abandon with a broken and contrite heart at the unadorned little altar. I fully accepted the reality of what Jesus had done for me, earnestly repented of my sin, and willfully tore the "No Vacancy" sign off my heart.

Jesus' words, "I am the truth, the way, and the life: no man comes unto the Father but by me" became a reality. He *is* the way to the Father. I had prayed many times previously, but my spirit had never truly penetrated into the presence of God. But now, after inviting Jesus into my life I was standing before the very throne of grace. This was truth. This is what life *is* all about. "What's going to happen after I die?" I am going to live in heaven forever. "Why am I here?" *To love God, and to share Him with others.* I know Him. I love Him. *HE IS REAL!*

Chapter 3

MY ENEMY HAS A NAME

Be sober, be vigilant; because your adversary the devil walks about like a roaring lion, seeking whom he may devour.

1 Peter 5:8

The tender love of Jesus began flowing through my entire being, creating a compulsive compassion to give. Often a sign of true repentance is when the Lord has control of your purse strings. When God said, "Give" I gave. We began by supporting a little South American girl through the Christian Children's Fund. This small act of obedience was the beginning of selling out to God. We had never given to the Lord before—what an unexpected joy!

Life was spelled c-o-n-t-e-n-t-m-e-n-t. We had Kimberly and our new baby boy, Kevin, to love; our marriage was the best ever; and I had a lifelong Friend—Jesus Christ. Eager to learn more and more about my Living Savior, and seeking to please Him became my lifetime motivation.

Mrs. Pollard, our 74-years-young Sunday school teacher, was a saintly lady who was instrumental in pointing me in the right direction. Her anointed teaching brought the Holy Scriptures powerfully alive in our everyday lives. Often I would pack up the babies and all their paraphernalia, and scurry over to her modest old-timey home to soak in her godly knowledge and wisdom in answer to my myriad of quick-fire questions. She had an amazing grasp of Biblical truths. Truths I had never heard before.

It amused me when Mrs. Pollard talked about the devil. "The devil was sitting on my shoulder this morning, whispering into my ear, trying to make me worry again," she'd retort, "but I just flicked him off, and told him to get out in the name of Jesus."

This concept of the devil was completely new to me. Laughingly I shared my ignorance, "I have always pictured the devil in a bright red suit with two horns and a pitchfork." "That's a dangerous image," she warned, "because it makes him seem to be a harmless joke. Satan wants us to pass him off as funny, or better yet, to believe that he doesn't exist at all." With a twinkle in her eye she challenged me. "You get into your Bible, and read what Jesus has to say about the devil. Believe me, he's real."

It did not take long to verify the reality of the devil, and he's not that cute little cartoon character either. Reading through the gospels I found that Jesus had real interaction, conversation, and confrontation with him on a regular basis. The disciples and the gospel writers also had much to say about his interference in people's lives, and gave priceless instruction as to identifying his methods and defeating his power.

These words of explanation are not to glorify satan, but to expose him and his tricky tactics. He is out to "steal, kill and destroy" (John 10:10). Jesus said, "I saw satan fall like lightning from heaven. Behold, I give you the authority to trample on serpents and scorpions, and over all the power of the enemy, and nothing shall by any means hurt you" (Luke 10:18–19). So we have nothing to be afraid of—Jesus has empowered us to stand against satan, but first we have to become aware that we have an enemy—that he is real and has real power; and then we must learn how to fight him.

In this section I am concentrating only on the revelation of spiritual warfare that was taking place in our lives at that specific time. In many ways we were fodder for the forager of our souls— ignorant, deceived and seemingly powerless in our understanding. But God was exposing us to His truth in ways we would never forget.

Obviously obedience is not one of the devil's virtues. Our obedience to Christ is a bitter pill for him, because he knows it will lead us to reality and ultimately to victory over our lives. His method of operation is to keep us deceived, self-focused, and/or hopeless. Thus, when we are obedient he's quick to attack us through circumstances that will discourage us or draw us off track. Deception is really the only power he has against Christians, but the more we hide God's Word in our hearts, the less we will be deceived. The more we know what God's Word says, the quicker we will be able to recognize the enemy's lies.

He wryly wraps sin in bright paper packages with colorful bows, and offers them to us with subtle phrases such as: "You deserve it." "You only live once." "Do your own thing." These phrases appeal to the ego and are powerful tools of the enemy that lead people astray. We believed his lies.

At this point in our lives John was not a Christian, and I was a baby in the kingdom with little knowledge of what the Bible said, so satan subtly drew our attention to a get-rich-quick business that tied us in knots for two years. This company skillfully misused the Scriptures by quoting such verses as Matthew 7:7, "Ask and it will be given to you; seek, and you will find; knock, and it will be opened to you." However, they ignored Matthew 6:33, "But seek you *first* the kingdom of God and His righteousness, and all these things shall be added to you." This experience of seeking earthly treasure brought barrenness to my soul. Life was becoming cluttered with the superficial.

There is no condemnation in the earning of large sums of money. John Wesley once said we should "earn all we can, save all we can, give all we can." But in our society money has become a god. People have become slaves to it, bow down and worship it. The materialism and humanism it affords usurps the place of God in many lives. Jesus said, "You cannot serve two masters; God and money. For you will hate one and love the other, or else the other way around." (Matthew 6:24,TLB)

These months of floundering between priorities found me doubting my salvation. Instead of a compulsive desire to give, I focused on a fantasy of accumulating wealth, which robbed me of much spiritual strength. Unfortunately we endured further disruption by being transferred to another city, leaving me completely drained and unprepared for Christi's birth, which was a particularly strenuous one.

Chapter 4

YIELDING CONTROL

However, when He, the Spirit of truth, has come, He will guide you into all truth.

John 16:13a

We were thrilled with the new little person God had miraculously created through us. I anxiously awaited the day of our release from the hospital, only to discover that Christi had jaundice and needed to remain under a special fluorescent light for several days.

Being completely wiped out physically, emotionally and spiritually I collapsed into the security of John's arms. "What is going to happen to our baby? I wanted to take her home." John was a Christian in name only, and yet he assured me that *his* God was big enough to handle the situation.

His words jolted my spirit. He was absolutely right—where was my faith? I was embarrassed before God, and felt that I had let Him down by acting flaky and spiritually weak in front of John. How was John ever going to come to know Jesus personally if I continued to be such a poor witness of His loving grace?

With a truly broken and contrite heart I called out to God confessing my unbelief and humbly repenting. From that moment a hunger and thirst to know more of my Savior, and to be spiritually stronger began to consume me. This all lead to our eventually evaluating our motivation for attending church. We wanted to learn more about the Bible, instead we were hearing social sermons. We wanted to learn more about Jesus Christ, but we were hardly hearing His name mentioned.

The thought of leaving our church was grievous to me, but we were dying of thirst, and there was nothing to drink. Being a people-pleaser, I did not want to hurt anyone's feelings, especially the pastor's, but when John asked me, "Do you want to please God, or man?" the answer could not be avoided.

I had heard of a good rule of thumb that might apply to this type of situation: if you are sitting on a keg of ice (a spiritually cold church) and the ice is melting, stay. If you are sitting on a keg of ice and freezing, leave. We were freezing.

The following Sunday morning we ventured a visit to our neighbor's church. The people evoked a down home warmness that encircled our hearts and embraced us like family. The pastor radiated the love of God, and his sermons fed my spirit week after week. Obedience had paid off.

"Evangelism Explosion" was a course being offered to help people share their faith. It was there that I found the terminology to describe what had taken place at the little altar in South Carolina— I had been *saved!* The previous denomination did not call it that, but nonetheless, that is what had happened to me. Now I wanted John and everyone in my family to have that understanding too. I ingeniously used them as my guinea pigs as I practiced sharing my faith with them. So at that point they were all at least giving mental assent to belief in Christ, and I am sure the Holy Spirit used it to plant and water some spiritual seeds. They all ended up being fed spiritually through regular church attendance.

REVIVAL: It was a word of the mysterious unknown to me. I really did not know what to expect, but was keenly curious. The evangelist was a sparkly white-haired lady who spoke with the authority of God. Each service found me perched on the edge of a front pew, soaking in every spirit-saturated word that flowed from her mouth. I diligently observed night after night as people's desire for the Lord was fervently renewed.

I had always known the proper terminology was "Father, Son, and Holy Spirit," but had never given much thought to the Holy Spirit being *a person*—that He wanted to have control of my life, or that He would empower me to live for Jesus.

The evangelist explained, "The Holy Spirit is already living within you if you are a Christian, but He is not free to work in your life unless you invite Him to have His way in you."

That night I knelt at the altar and told Jesus of my willingness to yield control of my life to the Holy Spirit. It was a simple action, void of emotion, but while returning matter-of-factly to my seat, the tears started gently trickling down my cheeks—still no feelings of emotion, just leaky eyes.

In the weeks following the revival there was a drastic change in my reactions. Previously I would break out in profuse perspiration if anyone even hinted at my taking responsibility in the church such as teaching Sunday school. But now I was bubbling with enthusiasm and eager to get involved.

My desire to give intensified upon hearing God's teaching on tithing. When I realized that we were actually robbing God (Malachi 3:8) by not tithing I shared my new understanding with John. His response: "Is that before or after taxes?" In startled encouragement I ran to phone our pastor. He did not hesitate to respond, "The government takes the cream of the crop—right off the top. I don't believe the Lord should receive anything less."

John agreed. Not only were we to give at least 10% of our income to the Lord from that point on, we also decided to catch up on our back tithe for the present year, which amounted to $1600. Not having that amount on hand, John went down to the bank and took out a loan for the first time in our lives. Our eagerness to obey was rewarded a couple months later when we received a surprise bonus that paid off our loan and provided for a new color television.

God is always faithful to His promises. "Give, and it will be given to you; good measure, pressed down, shaken together, and running over, will be put into your bosom. For with the same measure that you use it shall be measured back to you (Luke 6:38).

Enthusiasm welled within me. My confidence as a group leader was building. It did not seem threatening to me when asked to be a circle leader. I said yes, and yes again when asked to be the Spiritual Life leader of the Women's Fellowship. When leaders were needed for the Junior High Youth Group, I volunteered. To top it off they assigned me the fifth grade Sunday school class!

With a new baby and two preschoolers I had no business doing all of the above. This is what is called ignorance on fire. Certainly the Lord led me into a couple of these ministries, but I am sure He did not have a one-woman-band in mind. The evidence is clear. He blessed what He called me to, and He left me on my own with what I called me to.

The Sunday school class was a joy. Preparing and presenting the devotions for the Women's Fellowship was fruitful. The circle and the youth group had their problems. I quickly learned that if the devil cannot make you bad, he will make you busy. His accomplished goal is the same—to keep you out of God's perfect will.

I was in the process of learning that a *need* does not constitute a *call*. God would call me to certain tasks and I was not to feel guilty about not meeting other needs, no matter how pressing they may be. I needed to learn to listen for the Spirit's leading.

That summer we were privileged to attend a Family Life Seminar in which Dr. James Hatch talked about love American-style and love Biblical-style. He said that love American-style says, "My heart goes pitter patter. I can't eat. I can't sleep. I am in love as long as the object of my affection keeps meeting my needs, looking great, saying and doing all the right things . . . . But when the feelings leave that means I don't love him/her any more."

Love Biblical-style says, "Put on love" (Colossians 3:14). That is "put on" as you would put on a coat: you do it. It is a command from God. He is not saying, "I think you should," or "It would be nice if you did." He says, "Do it." God gives us the ability to do what He commands.

Hearing these and other basic Biblical truths did not automatically instill them into our marriage. They were as seeds scattered on the soil of our hearts, and it was the enemy's intention to swoop down like a starving vicious vulture and try to steal them from us. I realized that one of the ways that the enemy was stealing from our marriage relationship was through my busyness, as previously described.

Chapter 5

FROM FANTASY TO REALITY

John answered, saying to all, "I indeed baptize you with water; but One mightier than I is coming, whose sandal strap I am not worthy to loose. He will baptize you with the Holy Spirit and fire.

Luke 3:16

The Lord graciously removed me from this whirlwind of church busy-ness by transferring us to Charlotte. I did get involved writing curriculum and teaching a class for Bible Study Fellowship and a fifth grade Sunday school class, but my commitment outside the home ended there. Our move was initiated by John's company, which had decided to build a new plant in Charlotte, with John as the manager. This was a boyhood dream come true. He was not complaining about the substantial salary increase and classy car that came with it either!

John was decidedly intoxicated with himself for several months. Jeremiah 49:16 points out that the pride of our hearts deceives us—and he was a prime target. Believing he was king of the mountain and could do as he well pleased, he became involved in an adulterous relationship. John's unfaithfulness did not last long, however, because God in His mercy used this sin to bring him to salvation. For the first time in his life, John saw a picture of himself as a sinner in desperate need of the Savior.

We were working through the stress of moving so I did not pick up on any behavioral change as out of the ordinary, and this chapter of John's life would remain hidden from me for another two years. Our life together went on pretty much business as usual.

John was still on the road two nights a week. It was becoming harder and harder to see him go. His absence exacerbated my loneliness in this new environment. I resolutely worked at being independent (doing my own thing), while he was out of town, and when he returned my schedule was squelched. I would have to switch gears for a few days and adjust to his presence in our home, only to repeat the corroding cycle again four days later.

We settled Kevin into a four-year-old kindergarten at a nearby church, which drew our attention as a possible place of worship for our family. This stately two-hundred-year-old edifice appealed to our traditional backgrounds, so one Sunday morning we decided to attend services there. It did not take long to discern that the man in the pulpit loved Jesus Christ, and had a special relationship with Him.

Our hungry, disoriented hearts drew us back into the evening service where much to our surprise we found a completely different format from the traditional morning worship. The music was lead by a young lay couple. Fred played his guitar and led the singing, while Jenny accompanied him on the piano. Several people in the congregation played their tambourines as we sang songs from the Bible. This was a different worship format for us, but basically non-threatening. We clapped our hands and sang for about a half an hour, however, we began to get a little uptight when they kept singing "Alleluia" at higher and higher levels while raising their hands.

I knew this was scriptural because I had recently read in the Psalms of David worshiping in this manner (28:2, 63:4, 141:2, 143:6). Nevertheless, it was a little unnerving for us. It was later helpful to think of this action as a gesture of surrender—surrendering our ways for His.

The search for God's direction for us continued in the scriptures—maybe we had made a mistake in coming to Charlotte. "Jesus, was it really your voice we were listening to?" As I waited in His presence the tenth chapter of John came to my mind. At the time I had no idea what that chapter said. I grabbed my Bible and anxiously leafed through to the Gospel of John, the tenth chapter. The fourth verse caused my heart to leap! "And when he brings out his own sheep, he goes before them; and the sheep follow him, for *they know* his voice." Praise the Lord—we were in His will.

Every time we heard the pastor preach our spirits were stimulated. He walked close to the Lord and was sensitive to the Spirit. He preached about Jesus, and the power of the Holy Spirit, about the Baptism of the Holy Spirit, and walking in the Spirit.

We had never heard the term "Baptism of the Holy Spirit" before. It was explained to us that the Holy Spirit came to live within us when we received Jesus as our Savior, but like a guest waiting in the anteroom, the Holy Spirit was a gentleman and waited to be invited to make Himself at home.

One friend shared with me that I could make a fist and put my hand in a glove, but I would not be able to use my hand until I released my fingers to fill the whole glove. So it is with the Holy Spirit. He is in the believer's heart, but He needs to be released within to fill us with His power. Jesus is the one who baptizes us in His Spirit.

As I sought the Lord in the Scriptures I found in Acts 8:14-17 and Acts 19:1-6 examples of believers who had been baptized in the name of the Lord Jesus, however, they had not yet received the Baptism of the Holy Spirit. In Acts 8 Peter and John went to them and laid hands on them and they received the Holy Spirit, and in Acts 19 Paul ministered in the same way. This plainly confirmed to me that receiving Christ and receiving the Baptism of the Holy Spirit are two distinct experiences, although I understand that some people experience them at the same time.

Now I understood what had happened to me when I went forward at that revival I had attended years before. They had not put a label on what I had experienced—they did not even believe in the Baptism of the Holy Spirit, but we all knew something was different.

Jesus said, "If you, then being evil, know how to give good gifts to your children, how much more will your heavenly Father give the Holy Spirit to those who ask him?" (Luke 11:13). The

Holy Spirit will then empower us to do what God has planned for us to do.

John also experienced some spiritual breakthroughs in Charlotte. He received Jesus Christ as his Savior in his heart (about eighteen inches lower than his previous mental ascent) and he too was baptized in the Holy Spirit.

Chapter 6

A SURPRISE BAPTISM

So what do we do? Keep on sinning so God can keep on forgiving? I should hope not! If we've left the country where sin is sovereign, how can we still live in our old house there? Or didn't you realize that we packed up and left there for good? That is what happened in baptism. When we went under the water, we left the old country of sin behind; when we came up out of the water, we entered into a new country of grace—a new life in a new land!

Romans 6:1-4 (The Message)

Would we be interested in going to a Camp Farthest Out retreat? We had no idea what a CFO retreat was, but if Horace (our pastor) wanted us to be there, we wanted to be there.

On the last day of the retreat it was announced that Tommy Lewis was going to be baptizing people in the hotel's swimming pool that afternoon. Anyone who wished to participate was welcome. It was a glorious service. We sang and Tommy read the Scriptures about baptism as a symbol of the old self (our old naturally sinful way of living) being buried with Jesus and our new self (our new life), rising from the dead with Him. The Holy Spirit was convicting me as I cautiously watched, silently telling the Lord, "If I had an opportunity to talk to Tommy about this, I would."

At that instant the lady sitting next to me called him over. They talked for a few minutes while the Holy Spirit stirred up my courage. "Mr. Lewis, my husband and I were sprinkled when we were babies, but we haven't been baptized since we have met Jesus. Is it necessary?"

Tommy answered, "I believe that the very fact that you are asking me this is because the Holy Spirit wants you to receive the believer's baptism today, and I think you want to do it, don't you?" Before I had a chance to answer, John burst out, "Let's go!" as he dove into the pool. No more understanding was needed. I waded out into the waist-high water where John and I were baptized together as an outward expression of our inward transformation.

I had not counted on a dripping wet head that afternoon. Plans for the three o'clock session went out the window—my thick hair would never dry in time (This was before "blow dryer" became a household word). John went ahead to the session, only to return moments later with a woman he had met in the lobby. She was holding a blow dryer (I had never heard of, nor seen a blow dryer before this). "That's very thoughtful of you, but I don't know how to use one of those." "No problem," she chirped, "I'm a beautician. I'll do it for you."

About fifteen minutes later I was in my seat with a new hair-do and had not missed a word of the teaching. John said, "Don't you know you are a child of the King? When you obey Him, He takes care of all your needs." Praise the Lord!

The Lord touched John's life in a deep way that week. "He cried a lot, which was really unusual. I had not seen him cry since our honeymoon! I guess on our honeymoon he cried because of the burden he had taken on, and now he was crying because of the burden Jesus was taking off. He had never been a person who liked to show affection, but now he was hugging everybody. And he kept asking, "What is the baptism of fire?" He asked Horace, he asked spirit-filled friends, he looked up Scriptures on the subject— it fascinated him. I have an idea that this was the beginning of his baptism of fire.

A few days before we left for the retreat I had been impressed with a young man, Jim Hill, whom I had met at the pastor's house. When I looked into his eyes I could not help thinking that Jesus' eyes must look something like his. They had a special peace and gentleness about them. When he said he lived in Hendersonville, NC, I knew I would be seeing him again some day. A couple weeks after the CFO retreat we were in Hendersonville visiting John's parents. We decided to drop in on Jim and his wife, Kathy. We had a precious time visiting with this young couple that obviously loved the Lord.

We were about to leave when Jim received what he believed was a word from the Lord for John. "Prepare your heart for a ministry of fire." We sat there quiet on the outside, but our hearts were pounding. Tears welled up in John's eyes and mine. The presence of the Holy Spirit lingered among us. Jim spoke softly and cautiously. He said only time would tell if this were a true word from the Lord. Jim, of course, had no idea of John's deep desire to experience the baptism of fire.

As best I can tell, the baptism of fire is a sovereign work of the Holy Spirit that is associated with judgment and cleansing. Just as the burning bush was afire, but was not consumed, so John was being prepared for further cleansing and consecration.

Chapter 7

WHAT AM I SAYING?

*And they were all filled with the Holy Spirit, and
began to speak with other tongues, as the Spirit gave
them utterance.*

Acts 2:4

Another reality that confronted me in this season was that the
manifestation of "speaking in tongues" is an evidence of the filling
of the Holy Spirit. When I received the Baptism in the Holy Spirit I
began experiencing many exuberant times of praise and worship
that lead me into spiritual realms of glory where words were not
adequate to express the joy in my heart. I would often just giggle at
the sounds coming spontaneously out of mouth that sounded like a
baby's babbling. (Jesus said, "Out of the mouth of babes and
nursing infants You have perfected praise!" (Matthew 21:16). I
never gave these words any special scrutiny my—focus was on
worshiping God. I had not received any previous teaching on
"speaking in tongues" and consequently had no preconceived
ideas.

When we began worshiping in Charlotte we would hear others
praying in languages we could not understand and heard teachings
on speaking in tongues. Again I prayerfully searched the Scriptures
and found in Acts 3 and Acts 19 specific instances where people
spoke in tongues after they received the Baptism of the Holy Spirit.

Once convinced that this was of God, I yielded my tongue to the Lord—simply asked Him for a prayer language.

At first I received only four words. I prayed them over and over during my morning quiet times until one day I just felt plain silly. The enemy was mocking me, telling me I was making the words up, but my desire to receive everything the Lord had for me was strong. I decided to search what I believed to be God's voice further. As best I could, I sounded out the words and wrote them down: abluose, masada, petrichi, reglioni.

Ideally a trip to the local library to find some books on various languages would be helpful (religioni sounded Italian for religion???). However, we lived in a rural area and I had three small children in my constant care, which made it difficult to arrange a study time at the library—my old college dictionary would have to do! I eagerly and expectantly tried to find the English words, which would be spelled the closest to those on my list.

Abluose: *abluent*, any substance used for cleaning.
Mazada: *mazard*, a hard head.
Petrichi: *petrify*, rigid, inflexible
Religioni: *religion*

Interpretation:
Cleanse me of my hardheaded, rigid religion!!

Needless to say, I fervently prayed those four words daily.

After about a month or so, we had a missionary couple share on a Sunday night about their experience on the field when they received the Baptism of the Holy Spirit. Their denomination did not believe that this was a work of the Spirit, so it abandoned them—providing no financial, or any other kind of support for them in the foreign country where they had been faithfully serving for years. Their story was heartbreaking. In the midst of the pain and confusion that ensued, the husband began to doubt their whole experience. He stopped praying in his prayer language and was sinking into a depression.

During my quiet time the next morning I was deeply burdened for this man. I started out praying with my understanding, but soon became aware of rivers of living water flowing forth in the fluent expression of a new language. My breakthrough in speaking in tongues had come as I knelt at my bedside in intercession for a brother in Christ—how like the Lord to work in this beautiful way of weaving our lives with others.

It surely grieves the heart of God to see His children allowing the devil to bring division within His body over gifts that He Himself has bestowed. Paul said, "I wish you all spoke with tongues" (1 Corinthians 14:5). He continued in verse 18 to say, "I thank my God I speak in tongues more than you all." Does that sound like speaking in tongues is of the devil? Paul even exhorts Christians in verse 39, "Do not forbid to speak with tongues."

The devil cannot create a thing. His specialty is counterfeiting the gifts that God gives us. If our gifts and fruit are consecrated by the Spirit we have nothing to fear, and much to gain by obediently exercising them.

Chapter 8

MOVING ON

And everyone who has left houses or brothers or sisters or father or mother or wife or children or lands, for My name's sake, shall receive a hundredfold, and inherit eternal life.

Matthew 19:29

In July we visited my parents in Ohio. On the way home we lingered in Lexington, Kentucky on business. For four days John made sales calls for the company while the children and I enjoyed sunning and swimming in the motel pool. Both of us were aware of a strange, supernaturally familiar feeling that someday we would be living there. We reasoned the company would probably build a new plant in Lexington. This impression was so intense that upon our return home we assuredly announced to friends, "Don't be surprised if we get transferred to Lexington, Kentucky."

The Lord had been speaking to our hearts about giving away everything we had not used in the previous year, and to sell our house. At first we were skeptical of the latter instruction, but we did begin wistfully weeding through drawers, closets, the attic and other nooks and crannies where stored treasures were stashed.

My initial response to this trimming back was to compulsively cling to prized possessions like the tiny red velvet baby shoes that Kimberly and Christi wore on their first Christmases. "Oh Lord, I've just *got* to keep *them*!" The Spirit nudged me, "Think of the joy a young couple in Appalachia would experience slipping them on the tiny toes of their baby girl." As I thought about this couple the joy of giving welled up in my heart. I knew this would be pleasing to the Lord.

For days I had been curiously conscious of my diamond ring. It seemed that the Holy Spirit was gently inquiring if I could give it up. Later it was announced that the PTL Club was going to build a diamond house. Not a house built out of diamonds, but a house built by the money raised from auctioning diamonds that were being sent to the PTL ministry. My spirit quickened—this was where my diamond was to go.

When John came home I related the details, and he confirmed that we were to give the ring and my mink stole. We were well aware that the Lord was redirecting our lives, and we were offering this ring to Him in obedience to the Spirit. "But lay up for yourselves treasure in heaven . . . for where your treasure is, there will your heart be also." (Matthew 6:20, 21)

The Lord had initiated the prompting to sell our house in June, but neither of us believed we were hearing correctly, so we kept asking Him to speak louder! Six weeks later, after continual assurance, we believed Him. John and I have our morning devotions separately. He reads the books of the Bible at random. I begin January 1 systematically reading straight through, and yet we kept receiving the same message—often the same verses!

We did not know why we were to sell our house. We did not know where we were going, or what we were going to do, but we knew God was up to something. Once we had lightened our materialistic load, John sought our pastor's counsel concerning the house. Horace suggested we should put it on the market and see what happened. We had a little comfort in knowing the market was slow at this time. Humanly speaking a sale was doubtful.

Our house went up for sale on August 11th for the price that the Lord had impressed upon us. It was sold for that price on September 11th. We kept tugging on the Lord's coattail. Why did we have to sell our house? What were we going to do? Where were we going to live? He patiently repeated, "One step at a time. One step at a time."

Waiting is the tedious phase of obedience. It is during these waiting phases that we try to help God out by getting the action rolling on our own. The natural course seemed to be apartment or townhouse hunting. What a hectic mess! We were soon worn out and discouraged. The most frustrating roadblock was that we knew we were going to be involved in some kind of ministry, that we would not have an enormous income, but how much was "not much?"

Another obstacle was that John believed the Lord had a three-bedroom house or apartment for us to rent for $75 a month. I laughingly submitted an ad in the paper requesting the above mentioned specifications. No response.

In the midst of all this my friend, Benny, called bubbling with excitement, "We have had the most unusual happening in our household. Frank was taking a shower Tuesday morning when the Lord called him back to school and into the ministry! He finished most of his graduate work years ago. He has only one semester of classes to complete before graduation. He drove to Spartenburg and enrolled. The district superintendent gave us a church to pastor and a parsonage to live in. We'll be leaving in two weeks!"

I about fell over. "Benny, this is unreal. I can't believe how fast the Lord is moving. You have to come to dinner and fill us in on all the details!" The four of us kind of floated around all evening—thrilled that the Holy Spirit was transforming the lives of both families at the same time. Frank and Benny were talking up education. John chuckled, "It would have to be an act of God to get me back into school."

Within the week John was questioning a minister friend concerning the possibility of pastoring a church and finishing his education. Jeff responded, "Asbury . . . Asbury . . . Asbury." As John later drove into the driveway I vigorously motioned through the window that he had a phone call. He briskly rushed in and plopped a stack of books and pamphlet-type literature on the kitchen counter. While he was on the phone I curiously browsed through the intriguing assortment of texts. John had not read a book in ten years. Where in the world had he been?

Further examination revealed that they were all written by men from Asbury Theological Seminary. Leafing to the publishing information I discovered that the seminary was in Wilmore, Kentucky. It felt like a shot of electricity bolted through me— Wilmore *had* to be near Lexington! I scrambled around the house searching for a Kentucky map. Four maps into a pile I spotted Wilmore—fourteen miles south of Lexington.

John was still on the phone when Jeff appeared at our back door with the latest catalog on Asbury College housing. We anxiously flitted through and found that a three-bedroom duplex rented for $72 a month. Was that close enough? John immediately arranged a business trip to Lexington with Asbury College on the itinerary.

*   *   *   *   *

Noble oaks and maples with their rich fall colors shaded the sprawling front lawn that sloped from the administration building semi-circle to Lexington Avenue. It was a warm, yet stately setting. Was this to be our future home? The Director of Admissions, Dr. William Eddy, encouraged us to lay a fleece before the Lord as Gideon had done. If John was accepted academically, and we were assigned a three-bedroom duplex we would know that Jesus wanted us there.

Housing of any kind was a miracle at this time of year in Wilmore, and the waiting lists were long. But when Dr. Eddy called the housing department to put our name on the list he was surprised to learn that we would be first in line because a requirement for a three-bedroom duplex was three children, and not many students qualified.

It was lightening our load time again. We certainly were not going to need living room furniture *and* den furniture in the inevitable smaller quarters. We gave our living room furniture to a friend. When I asked him if he could use a riding mower his joy became effervescent. He and his wife had just bought their first house and they had a genuine need for both furniture and lawn mowers.

We had to vamoose. John's parents offered us their home for six weeks while they were in Florida. We loaded our remaining possessions—still enough to fill a U-haul truck, and headed for a layover in Hendersonville, believing God was leading us one step at a time. By the way, when we pulled the door down on the back of the truck there was not an inch of extra room. If we had not been obedient in our giving we would have had a major problem.

The Monday following our exodus John gave notice to the company. This was a tough assignment because Hendershot and

Smith and its subdivisions had been his whole life until recently, and in the natural realm the future was uncertain.

John had tried to cash in his stock the year before, but for some reason or other the transaction never materialized. Now arrangements were being made to pay us twice the amount we had hoped for per share, which would be enough for John's education and our living expenses until he graduated.

After obediently severing the materialistic ties of the past, the Lord opened the door to the future. John received a letter of acceptance from Asbury College and they had a three-bedroom duplex waiting for us.

PART II

HUMILITY and FORGIVENESS

Chapter 9

LEARNING TO FORGIVE

Forgive and you will be forgiven.
Luke 6:37

Bright and early on Friday, January 2, 1976 John reluctantly resumed his college career after a ten-year hiatus from anything in print! This was unequivocally not the desire of his heart, and after perusing several syllabi he became overwhelmingly heartsick.

As he dejectedly sauntered into the housing office to pay our first month's rent he questioned, "Lord, are you sure this is where I'm supposed to be?" The secretary pulled our payment card out of her gray metal file and efficiently replied, "That will be $75.75." After John caught his breath, he began praising the Lord for His assurance. (Remember our ad?)

It was a long, tense first quarter. John spent from 8 a.m. until midnight either in class or studying, day in and day out, for three months. Our time together was whittled down to hours of me reading his literature assignments to him or watching him study while I drifted off to sleep.

Our lives had truly been shaken and turned upside down. By April the dust of disorientation had pretty much settled. Nevertheless, there remained a gnawing restlessness within me that I could not identify. As an alternative to running in circles I sought counsel from our new pastor, David Seamands.

In the midst of explaining my unrest, David interrupted, "Kathy, I don't like your attitude about yourself. You've been putting yourself down ever since you walked in here." My reaction was one of startled bewilderment. He evidently was not paying attention! When he had his say I channeled the conversation back to my previous train of thought.

It did not take David long to zero in on the perfectionism that ruled me. "Are you trying to play God?" he asked, catching me completely off guard. I did not know the answer let alone know how to verbalize it.

My recovery from speechlessness had not progressed far, when David added, "I don't like your feelings about God." He went on to explain himself, but I could not take it in—the man just did not know me. He obviously did not understand. I verbally agreed to come back the following week, while simultaneously deciding to cancel the appointment at my earliest convenience.

However, as I began to do the homework David had assigned, things began to fall into place. Reading *Your God is Too Small* by J. B. Phillips revealed that I was a slave to the "false God of one hundred percent," wanting to be perfect for Him. My second assignment was to stop reading a top quality devotional that scrutinized my soul in such depth that my conscious perfectionism was using it to lash me into utter discouragement.

Next, I was to ask the Holy Spirit and John to help me check how often I put myself down. Much to our amazement, we found that I did this continuously. It was a subtle background to everything that proceeded out of my mouth.

Another assignment was to talk with Mariann, a young wife and mother, who was struggling with the same restlessness. There was great comfort in knowing that I was not alone in my frustration and perfectionism. The best part of our time together was the fun we had laughing at ourselves.

The last exercise that David wanted me to complete was to think about my gut feelings about God. He was not questioning my *theology*, but he sensed that my *feelings* about God were skewed. This appeared to be a rather simplistic rabbit trail at first. I knew that God was loving, kind, good, full of mercy and grace, however, it was becoming obvious that David knew what he was talking about, so I obeyed.

Two nights later I sat bolt upright in bed in the middle of the night. Fear trembled through my heart—fear of God the Father. It was painful to accept that this fervent negative emotion toward God had been hiding in my heart. I had known Jesus for six years and was baptized in the Holy Spirit. How could it be that I was afraid of the Father?

Confessing my fear to God the Father released His love, which cast out the fear. I began standing on 1 John 4:18, "There is no fear in love; but perfect love casts out fear." Paul declares in his second letter to Timothy (1:7), "But God has not given us the spirit of fear, but of power and of love and of a sound mind." That spirit of fear was dispelled as I received the perfect, accepting, compassionate love of God into my heart.

I gratefully and expectantly kept the second appointment with David, which proved to be just as productive as the first. Once he picked up on my resentment he started in with what sounded like the typical "couch" questions: "Did you have a happy childhood? Did you love your mother and father?" It seemed kind of hokey to me, but I decided to play along with him. "I had a great time." He probed further, "Is there anything in your childhood that makes you feel resentful to remember—any particular incident?"

My first response was a firm "No." Then suddenly a scene came to my mind for the first time in years. My body tensed up as the memory surfaced, tears began to flow. "Now tell me what you are feeling—not as the grown up Kathy who is sitting here in my office, but the little girl Kathy who is experiencing pain." This was a dramatic experience—something you would see on the Monday night movie, but not something you would live through.

The scene that flooded my mind and emotions instantaneously had taken place when I was twelve years old. I had wanted to become a member of the Y-Teens group, a wholesome program sponsored by the local YMCA. Several of my friends were excited about joining, so one day after school I attended one of their meetings.

My mother had been a Girl Scout leader for several years, and most recently the leader of my troop. I had lost what little interest I had in scouts long ago, and was ready for a change, however, my desire to change streams was received by my mother as the ultimate insult. She interpreted my actions as an ungrateful personal betrayal.

We were standing out in the front yard of a friend's house when she learned of my exploration. She spontaneously ignited into a frenzied shouting tirade with her arms flailing uncontrollably through the verbally charged air, chasing me around the yard slapping me whenever she could make contact. I felt like I was running for my life, but there was nowhere to go, nowhere to hide. I covered my head with my arms lifted up and ran in circles, totally humiliated and ashamed—for her as well as for myself. This was all acted out in front of everyone on the block plus a multitude of onlookers driving by on the busy street.

Once I had poured out my painful story David asked, "Are you willing to forgive her?"

"I don't know."

"Are you willing to be made willing?"

"Yes."

I do not know how long he worked and cried with me that life-changing afternoon, but by the time it was over David's compassion and wisdom had drawn a lifetime of heartache out of me. Before we prayed he instructed me to paint a mental picture of a huge trash barrel marked **RESENTMENT** sitting at the foot of the cross. Every time the Holy Spirit revealed resentment in my life I was to throw that resentment into the barrel, and give it to Jesus. This image has been a tremendous tool in countless situations through the years. I recommend it to anyone dealing with the three cousins of unforgiveness, resentment, and bitterness.

The next two days found me physically exhausted with nausea, pounding headaches, and an aching in my arms and legs that were too heavy to lift. That childhood memory had been piercing my heart all those years—to the point that when I finally released it my whole body reacted. I will never forget the physical grip that unforgiveness held over me. My body was like a rubber band that is stretched to its limits, and when it is released it falls limp.

Doctors have confirmed that our hospitals are full of people who are there with bodies racked in pain because of the undetected death-grip that unforgiveness has on them. These negative emotions are powerful tools of the enemy to attack our whole beings. We must ask the Lord to reveal any of roots of bitterness, confess them as sinful, and repent of harboring them in our hearts. His love is then able to bring healing and restoration.

The months that followed were a continuous exercise in forgiveness. Old and new grievances, major and minor hurts one after another had to be brought to the barrel. Resentment had colored my relationship with almost everyone, and had had me emotionally bound. Someone once said, "Forgiveness is the perfume that the trampled flower casts back upon the foot that crushed it." That is the path I chose. I would never let the negative power of unforgiveness build in my life again. My heart was set to be a quick forgiver.

Chapter 10

FACING THE REALITY OF A FAULTY MARRIAGE

Except the Lord builds a house, they labor in vain who build it.
Psalm 127:1

JOHN:

I met Carol in my philosophy class during the spring quarter. I noticed her right off because she looked like my wife. We had a lot in common, being older students, each with three children about the same ages. So it was easy to talk with each other.

One day Carol came into class all excited. She and her husband had just been to a marriage enrichment weekend, and it had quite an impact on their marriage. They were now able to talk about their feelings and thoughts as never before—a new life was opening up for them. Carol cautiously shared that her marriage had been in a state of separation and that the weekend had brought them back together. She had learned that his reason for the separation had been his involvement with another woman. He examined his ways, repented and wanted to make a go of their marriage. As a result they were communicating for the first time in years.

But now their time was up. He was in the armed services and was heading overseas for six months. Only days after their reconciliation the joy of their newly found communication was dissipating. Doubts and fears were flooding in on her as the pressure of taking care of their three children alone, and going to school full time overwhelmed her. I listened. I understood. We prayed.

That night I related the day's events to Kathy. She was quite quick to warn me not to continue this sharing, sensing that there was a need for caution. But at that time I felt no danger. Over the weeks I saw Carol become strong again. We talked daily. It all seemed very natural. Then suddenly I realized that I was overly attracted. The friendship had taken a turn into infatuation. I was in trouble and I knew it.

Through prayer the Lord led me to fast. My feelings for Carol were strong, but God had joined me with Kathy in marriage forever, "until death do you part." It became clear that I needed to transfer these feelings back to Kathy, where they belonged. My true need to give love was really a need to give to my wife. I was holding a love inside me that needed to be released.

I had a vision of what our marriage could be. I would be able to look into her eyes and know how she felt. I would be sensitive to her hurts, her desires, her needs, and be able to share mine with her. I knew there was a level of intimacy that we were missing, and I desperately wanted to find it.

I spent the week fasting and praying that the Lord would show me how to get my life in order. I wanted to love Kathy with my whole heart. The Lord showed me that week that our marriage was not the exception. Many of our friends also felt that marriage had to be better than what they were experiencing. I knew God was saying that He wanted me to help free His people from satan's trap of mediocre marriage—that He had something better.

The week of fasting had been a painful time of facing truth. My selfishness ways began to surface. I had thought that I had done a great service for the kingdom of God by selling my house and my part of our family business to go back to school and follow Jesus after ten years in the business world. But I never felt the pain of real sacrifice. Now Jesus was saying, "John, you are self-centered. Your world revolves around you. You want to have life your own way." What was the Lord asking of me? Did He expect John Hendershot to not just follow Him, but give up his whole self? Yes. He was telling me to get my mind and my life tuned back in on Him—to get my family and my marriage back where they needed to be.

The week was full of water works. I would wake up with tears running down my face. When I was in prayer I cried. If I was not crying I wanted to be. I felt the need to cry. I guess I was mourning my own death, because I knew I had to change to get right with Jesus or continue to be miserable.

Friday came and the fast was over. I had asked Kathy to go out to dinner with me. I attempted to lineup a babysitter, and make all the arrangements, which I usually expect her to do. I picked a quiet, expensive place to spend the evening. We had what appeared to be a leisurely dinner, but I could not say much without filling up with tears. I wanted to be close, but my own walls kept us apart. It had been so long since we had been alone that I did not know what to do with myself. Whenever we had had time together we had always been busy doing things—going shopping, or being with our family or friends. We actually spent very little time alone. It made me wonder what people did alone. What did they talk about? How did they feel?

It came to mind that the need to give was one of the first things I wanted to fulfill when we first met. I used to send her cards and short letters, little things. Over the years this had been cast aside. Since this was the Saturday before Mother's Day, I decided to send her a dozen red roses. When they were delivered she lit up like she used to. A sixty-thousand-dollar diamond could not have received a more appreciative welcome.

I was aware of a need for change in our relationship because I had experienced an openness with Carol the way I had once related with Kathy. We needed this openness back in our marriage. That Sunday became a day of gut level sharing—more than we had done in years. I felt like I was setting a match to our marriage, but something compelled me to get out my frustration. It seemed as if we were playing a game called "Marriage" taking on roles and holding back emotions.

I needed to hold Kathy. Just to have her in my arms meant everything. As she slipped into my arms there was a release of power, and a joy of fulfillment even though my tears ran like rivers. It is still amazing to me as I recall crying. I had never been free to cry in front of anyone. Now I cried in class, at home, anywhere and everywhere. The Spirit of God allowed me to experience this freedom without embarrassment.

The Sunday of tears and talking about what marriage should be like was a step toward repenting of a wall of pride. It was my fault that Kathy was not meeting my need. She was responding to me only as I would let her. I had not shown her much of the true John for years. I had been in a profession where to keep secrets was good business. This became a way of life for me, a pattern, which over the years covered my insufficiencies and my emotions, resulting in a hard shell protection of my inner life. For years I had not expressed my joys, my sorrows, or my anxieties with Kathy, and now I did not know how.

The Lord was telling me to end the relationship with Carol. To end it without a word of explanation seemed wrong to me, even though the Bible says to flee temptation. I was weak and ego was still in control of my actions. I wanted it both ways. I was standing on a moving boat with one foot in the boat and the other on the dock—unaware of how wet I was going to become within the next forty-eight hours.

I told Kathy I had to get away for the day. I told her I needed to stop by the library, shop for some clothes and just be by myself. She objected. It was as if she knew I was about to fall into a bear trap, and she wanted to save me from the pain, but there was no stopping me. My real plan was to go to Carol's on Monday and end our relationship. I never expected to have my life changed in such a drastic way. I did not foresee the pain and sorrow ahead, or the darkness that was closing in on me.

KATHY:

I could not believe the words that were penetrating my eardrums—they seemed unreal. "A couple of years ago I was ready to chuck our marriage and the only reason I didn't was because of my relationship with the Lord." I could not believe this was *my* husband talking about *our* marriage. We had a good solid marriage—everybody knew that. What in the world was he talking about?

John had had a long spiritually strenuous week of fasting, praying, and crying. I knew the Lord was dealing with him so I was not overly concerned. He was in good hands. He did say that the Holy Spirit had shown him that he had been neglecting me. Because of that revelation John had taken me to a top-notch steakhouse the previous Friday night. He had been quiet and teary eyed, but we still had a pleasant evening.

Saturday had been another low-key day. John was silently sitting in the living room recliner with tears dripping down his face. I sat at the table with the children, trying to eat my baloney sandwich, but it did not want to go down. There was a big lump in my throat that made swallowing a physical feat. With long hard gulps some chunks dropped down my gullet, but halfway through I gave up.

I had no words of comfort for him. I went over and curled up on his lap with my head on his shoulder for about an hour. I just wanted to be close to him. As his tears dripped down his cheeks and onto mine, down my face and under my chin, I did not move to brush them away. Somehow that would have ruined the preciousness of the moment. It was a precious closeness, sacred, as if the Lord were baptizing our marriage, our oneness, with John's tears.

Later Saturday afternoon John told me he had to get out of town for a day. He felt hemmed in. He made plans to pick up a book for one of his classes, but more importantly, he needed time to be alone. That rejection hurt. He was shutting me out again. But after a few complaining remarks, a friend accused me of being possessive, so I stifled my objections.

About an hour later a dozen long-stemmed red roses were delivered. They were from John for Mother's Day. Needless to say, my emotions were pretty well strung out by this time. My release came in the form of a good cry!

What did all that mean? As we sat on the couch talking and crying all Sunday afternoon there was a gentle spirit flowing. We sat close together. John's arm was around me. We often hesitated in speaking out because our eyes regularly filled with tears. We were a living example of what the Bible calls "speaking the truth in love."

John continued, "There is a love that you have suppressed in there (pointing to my heart), and it's mine, and I want it." With that statement he reached toward me as if he were grabbing that invisible love from my heart and putting it into his. He said, "Yesterday afternoon when you came and sat on my lap I saw a side of your love that I have never seen before. That's the side of you I want."

I could understand the words that he was saying although I was not sure what they meant, or what either of us might do about them. My mind was groping for answers. Was I suppressing love? How? Why? I had always had a fear of John's death and had recently been counseled about it. Could that have something to do with this "suppressed love?" "I have always been afraid to surrender my love completely to you because I was afraid if I became dependent on you, and then you died, I would be completely lost." John immediately responded in a firm voice, "Well girl, wait until I am dead to mourn me. Don't mourn me now while I am still alive!" I could not help wondering where in the world that thought came from. Was that really what was going on?

As we sat there talking, listening, crying my mind was asking a million questions. My heart was crying out to Jesus to be with us as old securities were being threatened. I had prided myself on being a good wife, having a good marriage. I had listened to John's problems, moved with him from city to city as we were transferred every two years, and I had kept up my personal appearance. My housekeeping had not been condemned by the department of health. I had taken care of our children, been faithful, and had enjoyed our physical relationship when there was time. What were we talking about? I really was not sure that night.

A lot of important things that needed to be said were said, but I was totally void of physical and emotional strength to figure out what they were. Thank the Lord sleep came instantly as I laid my head on my pillow, because I was going to need it.

Chapter 11

IN THE MIDST OF THE STORM

But God is faithful [to His Word and to His compassionate nature], and He [can be trusted] not to let you be tempted and tried and assayed beyond your ability and strength of resistance and power to endure, but with the temptation will [always] also provide the way out (the means of escape to a landing place, that you may be capable and strong and powerful to bear up under it patiently.

1 Corinthians 10:13b (Amplified)

<u>JOHN:</u>

I can remember awaking refreshed that Monday morning, and feeling like the world was a great place to live. I showered, dressed and took our son to school, and then headed for the city. The car was just out of the auto repair and was tuned to precision. The power under foot felt exhilarating that sunshiny morning, as I drove off confidently to complete my mission. My relationship with Carol would be behind me, and my life would be straightened out with God. These were my thoughts as I pulled up in front of Carol's house that morning.

After exchanging greetings we talked about the fact that we could not continue to see each other. We were giving time and feelings to each other that belonged to her husband and Kathy. As Christians we knew that this was wrong. We asked the Lord Jesus to forgive our sins of feelings, thoughts, and time spent together. It was a long prayer. We asked Jesus to keep us in His light and let us see His will. We thanked Him for showing us His power in our lives.

I left Carol's and went to a nearby park to read and pray and just spend a few quiet hours with the Lord. God's presence was real. I was free for the first time in weeks—no guilt, no anxiety, just the peace of knowing I was walking as my Maker designed me to walk. I picked up my book, grabbed a quick lunch and started home to the family I had been depriving of my true self for years, determined to be a new person, totally committed to lead and serve them.

When I arrived home the conversation quickly turned to the subject of the day's events. Suddenly Kathy sensed that I might have gone to see Carol. She came right out and asked if I had. When I answered the world began to cave in on top of me.

Kathy had good reason to be angry and non-understanding of what I had done. She asked why I went. I could not give an answer. I felt helpless. I had no answer. It was as if my mind were a blank. "Oh Lord, why? I have done what you asked. I have given up ego and pride. I have surrendered to Your will. Why, when it seems so right is it feeling so wrong?"

Kathy was upset. She was so upset it seemed like our whole life could be affected for years to come. I was scared. I tried to be close to her. I tried to talk, but could not. Nothing would come out. My mind was thinking the worst. How would life be without my family? I had never been faced with the importance of the whole family being together. Now I thought about how terrible it would be to lose them.

At six-thirty Kathy went to her sign language class. It was unusual for her to take the car instead of walking and she was leaving a half-hour early. I had put the kids to bed, and for some reason I felt that I would never see them again. I kissed each one and held them tight. My tears flowed. My heart ached. My mind was confused. I sat down and tried to think.

It was if the Father had turned His back on me. I was alone. Kathy was gone—maybe forever. I did not know. I felt like the kids were going to be leaving soon too. God had surely forgotten me. How could I feel this way if He were with me? I ran to the couple next door and asked them to take care of the kids. Without explanation they came over.

Where could she be? I ran to the building where her class was being held, but she was not there. The car was not on the street. Who would she go to? Louise was the logical one. By this time I had to walk because of shortness of breath—huffing like a steam engine as I prayer-walked the two blocks into town. There was the car! I ran up the two flights of stairs and knocked at the door. Someone said, "Come in."

There was Kathy. As she looked up I saw surprise on her face and a smile. I was repentant, and the whole world was not too large of an audience. I knew that Kathy was more important to me than my pride and ego could ever be. She was chosen for me by God, and I now knew what she meant to me. I could not believe that she had forgiven me! After a time of prayer and praise with the Moores we returned home.

I am not sure why all this happened, but God's grace was with us that night. Kathy had a love for me that only God could have given her after the events of that day. We were aware of each other as a gift from God. He showed us a new and better way in His love and gentleness.

KATHY:

As Louise descended the church stairs that Sunday morning I felt led to invite her to come over and spend the day with me on Monday. John was going to be gone all day so I might as well have some fun too!

Shortly after John left for his day alone, Louise arrived. I lost no time in pouring my heart out to her, describing the conversation John and I had had on Sunday afternoon—how unreal it all seemed to me. Louise sat compassionately nodding and encouraging me to get it off my chest. I could tell she was really empathizing. Little did I know that the Lord was ministering to her at this point. Louise could identity with much of what was being said, (when she went home she and her husband, Jack, had a time of confessing, forgiving, and cleansing before the Lord).

As Louise and I shared on into the afternoon we decided that there must be other women who looked happy, well adjusted, successful on the outside, but hurting, lonely and frustrated on the inside. We decided to pray about it and see if the Lord would have us start a small fellowship that would meet regularly to share needs and pray for each other.

The day seemed to slip away as we shared and ministered to one another. Around two o'clock John drove in. I had not expected to see him until dinner, so I was encouraged that he came home early. Louise left shortly after John came home. I began to share our conversation with him. I felt secure in God's love. I knew that Jesus had sent Louise my way, and now John was home. "Louise and I have decided to get together regularly and pray about starting a prayer and share group. We think there are other women who have similar needs for fellowship and support."

"That sounds like a good idea. I think you should invite Carol to join you. She's going through some hard times right now and she needs a friend." Carol? Carol? Fear gripped my heart. Prior to that moment I had never dreamt that he might have gone to see her. My heart kept whispering, "Jesus, I need You. Be here with us Lord. Stay with us." I was afraid to ask the question. Afraid of what the answer might be.

"Did you go to see her today?"

"Yes." (Oh my heart!)

"At her house?"

"Yes."

Oh God, what's going on? This can't be happening to *me!*

"Why did you go there?"

"I went to talk with her. Pray with her."

"About what?"

"About us. I wanted her to pray for us. She is going to visit a friend of hers who is thinking about asking her husband for a divorce and she wants me to pray for her."

"You had to go to her home to pray with her? Why didn't you meet her at the school or the church?"

No answer.

"What else did you do?"

"Nothing. I didn't give her anything that belongs to you except time."

That was a relief.

There was a long painful pause.

"I trusted you! I didn't like you going off by yourself today, but I trusted you."

The conversation was over. I could only sit and cry. I knew it hurt John to see me so crushed. It was as though he were feeling it with me. He tried to comfort me, to hold me. But I was so confused, dumbfounded, scared and hurt. I did not know what to do. I wanted to be alone.

I sought refuge in our son's room, but John followed me. I went out on the front porch. John followed. I went out on the back porch. He followed me again. There was no nook or cranny to hide in. I felt so sorry for him. He wanted to comfort me, but I needed to be alone to think.

We did not believe in divorce. That was not an option (we truly thank God that this was deeply instilled in both of us). I loved John. I did not want to leave him, but maybe I should go away for a little while until I could understand what was going on. He kept saying he loved me. How could I believe him? Why did he go to see her?

I thought we were starting on a new plain after yesterday's speaking the truth in love. "Oh Jesus, hold us up. I know You know what is going on. You understand it all. I know You can work even this to our good. Thank You for the assurance of Your love, Your power. Thank You for the reality of Your presence within me right now. Hold me tight Lord, don't let me slip away from You."

John had told me about Carol and her marital problems about a month before. I was concerned for her too, but had cautioned John about counseling her. She needed to talk to an older man or a woman. I was willing to talk with her. Why had he not listened to me?

After spending a couple of hours trying to dodge John and the children, somehow I managed to get dinner on the table. John and I sat on the back steps in silence while the kids ate. The tears came and left. Soon it was time to get ready for my sign language class. I had no intention of going but it was an excuse to get out of the house. I needed to talk to somebody. Louise was my obvious choice since she knew all about what had been going on with us.

Louise and Jack were expecting company who were running twenty minutes late when I arrived (we later agreed it was part of God's perfect timing because I would not have intruded if they had had company). When Louise opened the door I staggered into their apartment and sobbed for about ten minutes. She sat there quietly telling me to take my time, and let it all out. I knew she was praying for me.

Eventually I composed myself enough to tell her the latest revelations. Louise asked if I would be willing to tell the whole story to Jack, who had been in another room. I did not mind. It all seemed so unreal. It was as if I was listening to someone else talking. Jack listened carefully and prayerfully.

"Kathy, can you forgive John?"

"I don't know. It's not my nature to forgive. I just spent the last two months counseling with David over resentments that I've held for years. I *want* to forgive him, but I'm not sure I can."

Jack continued in his gentle way. "You know those Israelites went around that mountain and God said, 'Are you ready to forgive?' The Israelites said, 'Lord, you know it is not our nature to forgive.' They went around the mountain again, and the Lord said, 'Are you ready to forgive?' The Israelites said, 'Lord you know it is not our nature to forgive,' So they went around again." Jack had made his point.

As he was talking to me, I was talking to God in my heart, "Father, I don't want to go around this mountain again. I don't want to start building resentments again. I'm willing Lord to surrender this whole thing to you."

Jack was not quite through talking when there was a knock at the door. It was John. He came storming in with tears brimming over his eyelids. "I've come to repent. I was wrong and I'm sorry. I love you."

At that point I rejoiced in the faithfulness of my Lord Jesus. His timing is perfect. I had just turned everything over to Him and instantly the pain, the resentment, the confusion were gone. It was a miracle. I was enveloped in the peace that passes understanding. When I shared with the three of them what had just happened in my heart we all joined hands and praised the Lord!

Chapter 12

KEEP HOLDING ON

"Lord, how often shall my brother sin against me, and I forgive him? Up to seven times?" Jesus said to him, "I do not say to you, up to seven times, but up to seventy times seven."

Matthew 18:21–22

The Carol incident was over now, and we were both emotionally wiped out. Our Father, who knows all things from the beginning to end, knew what a strain we had been under, and what was yet ahead of us. Because of His loving concern He gave us a change of scenery and a change of pace that summer as we traveled, visited friends and relatives, and camped—wearing out our bodies and restoring our emotions.

It was good to get back to Wilmore in the fall, and get everyone back into a routine. Life seemed to be settling down for about a month before the dam broke loose again and the past came rushing over us like a flood.

For a couple years John had been covering up his unfaithfulness. He had confessed to Jesus. He repented and knew that Jesus had forgiven him, but he carried the secret guilt in his heart. The enemy used this guilt to build an invisible mountain between us without either of us realizing that the color of our marriage was fading. It was this black seed of the past that opened the door for the upheaval we had gone through in the spring with Carol and it finally erupted to the surface in the fall.

Over Labor Day weekend we went to Ohio to celebrate our eleventh anniversary with my parents, however, I was still feeling the affects of the flu so we did not celebrate. Even though I was feeling kind of rough physically, I felt loving toward John and tried to express that to him several times. Some bug bit him around suppertime and he started grumping at me for everything I did, or did not do, or say. The air conditioner was on in the guestroom, which made it too cold for me. I refused to sleep in there unless he turned it off—he left it on full force. For the first time in our married life he let me sleep on the couch by myself.

The next morning I could not get out of there fast enough. I was so hurt and angry with him I was about to pop, but I did not want to make a scene in front of my parents. They were already upset with me over my obvious silent treatment toward John that morning. I thought and prayed all the way to Columbus (about two hours into our trip home). By the time we hit Cincinnati (another two hours down the road) we had made up. But this acting out was just the tip of the iceberg. It was a sign that things had only been on simmer for the summer and we were creeping back up to a full boil.

Two days after school started I was ironing one afternoon when the phone rang. It was Carol's husband calling collect for John. I accepted the charges wondering why he would be calling. Carol's husband informed me that John had just called Carol and she had hung up on him. She and her husband were quite upset. They did not want any trouble between them as they were trying to make a new start. Her husband told me of a letter that John had written to her saying that he missed her. He had gone by her house and phoned her but no one was there (Carol's husband had moved back from overseas and they had moved out of state).

My mind whirled and my stomach wound into knots as I listened to the irate voice on the other end of the receiver. I thanked him for calling and assured him that John would not be causing him any more trouble. Surprisingly enough I had heard a sweet, understanding voice coming out of my mouth. As I hung up I realized that my body was trembling.

I picked up the phone once more to call David. I heard my inner voice saying, "Don't panic. John needs you to be strong." I could not understand what that meant, but I kept hearing it over and over. God's timing was once again perfect. David had just stopped by the office for a moment to pick up the mail. He was available to come over and talk with me.

David walks so closely with the Lord that just to have him come over was a comfort. He helped me put away some fears, and he echoed my inner voice, "Don't panic. John needs you to be strong for him." We prayed together and David suggested that John and I make an appointment to counsel with him together.

After he left I asked my neighbor to stay with the children while I walked down to meet John at the library. I sat on a bench outside waiting for John to exit. "Don't panic. John needs you to be strong for him. Don't panic" kept running through my mind. It seems ironic that I happened to be reading in the Book of Job. I could identify with Job. I sat meditating on Job and praying.

When John came out he was all smiles, seemingly very much at ease. I would have never known anything was wrong to look at him. "Hi, where are the kids?"

"They're at home."

"What are you doing here?"

"I came down to meet you. I felt we had some things to discuss without the kids being around."

"Oh, what's going on?"

"You tell me."

"Nothing" he said while shaking his head.

"John, *I know.* And I want you to tell me what's going on."

"Well, I called Carol this afternoon, but nothing happened. She hung up."

"Why did you call her?"

"I just wanted to make sure she was alright, and that she and her husband were happy. I knew I shouldn't have called. I resisted satan's whispers for a while. He kept saying, 'you're a Christian aren't you? Christians are supposed to love each other, aren't they?' After I called her, I went over to the chapel and prayed. The Lord told me that I have a big ego problem and that I was being disobedient."

The tears that had not come before, now trickled slowly down my lowered face and stopped as gently as they had begun. I told John about the phone call, word for word. I told him I wanted us to go to see David together. He agreed. The Lord silently ministered to us as we walked home.

During the next couple days I stuck closer than usual to the Lord. "When is all this going to end? Will I *ever* be able to trust him again? Why am I being strong for him?" Over and over questions answered with His strength, His love, His assurance that He was in control. At that time I was studying Billy Graham's *Discovery 2*. I was reading Job 22:21–26. The title of Wednesday's study was "Facing the Real Problem." As I read the scripture that morning I asked God to reveal my real problem, and he did.

> Yield now and be at peace with him; thereby good will come to you. Please receive instruction from His mouth, and establish His words in your heart. If you return to the Almighty you will be restored. If you remove unrighteousness far from your tent, *and place your gold in the dust,* and the gold of Ophir among the stones of the brooks, then the Almighty will be your gold and choice silver to you. For then you will delight in the Almighty and lift up your face to God (New American Standard).

"Place your gold in the dust," seemed to jump out at me. Gold. "What's my gold, Lord?" PRIDE became a neon light in my mind's eye. Pride is my treasure, my gold. Pride in the fact that He had worked and was working in my life; pride in what I thought was my humility, pride in my walk of forgiveness. These were gifts from God, and I was thankful, but I found myself being proud as if I created them or earned them. Yes, the Lord was dealing with both of us. These scenes were taking place for both of us to repent, to learn and to grow. The prayer at the end of this devotion asked for insight for discerning a person's real needs. This was my prayer—for insight into John's needs.

We were to see David on Friday afternoon. I had been fervently praying and continued to pray and fast on Friday, asking the Lord to surround David's office with His angels that the enemy could not touch us as we talked. I asked Jesus to reveal *anything* that we needed to look at, that nothing would be concealed. I had felt that John had a deep resentment toward me that he was not conscious of.

Most of the conversation was between John and David. I prayed silently and listened. David asked questions, but we did not seem to be getting anywhere. Then out of the clear blue, John dropped the bombshell. He had been unfaithful to me two years before. I almost passed out the shock was so great. In fact, it took me twenty-four hours to regain my strength. My mind went blurry as a myriad of feelings bombarded me with a relatively short amount of time—fear, anger, hate, rejection, bitterness. Physically it must have been something like a heart attack as far as the pressure on my chest, not being able to breath normally, being nauseous, feeling faint, going limp. My heart cried out, "It is over!"

John was relieved of two years of torment. His pressure was off. After we heard all the details David asked him to go home, but he kept me and counseled with me. I do not remember what we talked about exactly, but they were all the right words. Most importantly he was giving of himself to me. He was hurting with me, crying with me. In his compassion he was sharing my heartbreak. Some time later he drove me home.

All through the summer God had kept telling me to "hold on." Now I understood that these were words of preparation. My heart seemed like it was shredded into millions of tiny pieces. I wobbled straight into our room and fell onto the bed where I prayed quietly in the spirit for a couple hours. After John put the children to bed he stalked in and pulled the rocking chair up to the side of the bed. I stared up into his eyes. He seemed distant, emotionless, like a child steeled for punishment.

"Why are you staring at me?" he asked.

"Because I love you."

His defenses melted immediately. He wept. That was the beginning of the most tender season of our entire marriage.

As I continued my study in Job 28 on Saturday morning, once again the Holy Spirit ministered to me. "Try to leave this to the wisdom of God. Put God first, place all your trust in Him—that's the secret of true wisdom."

God had allowed the incident with Carol to take place to prepare me for this, and to show John that I could forgive. He had also allowed the telephone episode to prove to John the depth of my ability to forgive, which freed him to tell me the most difficult thing he has ever had to tell me. John needed the assurance first (and Jesus had to gradually establish that forgiveness within me). That is why Jesus kept whispering, "Don't panic. John needs you to be strong. Keep holding on."

Even though I did not want John to ever touch me again, the very next morning I dressed and was lying weakly on the bed, and John came in to lie next to me. He held me most of the day. There was little talking. I did not understand what was happening. I just wanted him to hold me.

It was like Jesus in him was healing me, and Jesus in me was healing him. I cannot explain it except that I know that touching is vitally important. We need to touch not only our spouses, but also our children and our friends. There is something powerfully impacting in a tender touch.

Dr. Wheat says that the need for touching is more basic than the need for sex. The reason we have such a sex-oriented society is that people are looking for that touching and the only way they know to get it is sex. What they are really looking for is a loving touch, a loving hug.

The giving of time was precious. We spent the whole day holding each other. Of course this was a crisis situation, but time is another essential in building and maintaining a healthy relationship. It takes time to edify. The Bible speaks of building up the body, edifying each other—that means giving each other healing attention—and that takes TIME.

We had made plans to go to a dinner meeting with several other couples that night. I thought, "There is no way we can go. We'd better call and tell them that we can't make it." But as the day went on this healing was taking place, and if there was any place that I wanted to be it was with God's children, singing His praises.

Incredibly enough I went feeling like a queen. John held onto me as if he were going to lose me. I knew that he loved me and now there was nothing hidden between us. It was such a relief after the previous two years. We were truly one. It was like living in a miracle because Jesus was so real to each of us directly as well as indirectly through each other.

As the soloist sang "To God Be the Glory" tears of thankfulness seeped through my closed eyelids and my hands lifted in praise. The speaker exalted the Lord and shared the miracles Jesus had manifested in his life. I inwardly shouted "AMEN!" throughout his testimony. Our God is a MIGHTY GOD! On the way home we sang along with a praise tape. It was glorious. LOVE had lifted me. Jesus turned my sorrow into joy.

Chapter 13

A NEW RED DRESS

*But if we walk in the light as He is in the light, we have
fellowship with one another, and the blood of Jesus Christ His
Son cleanses us from all sin.*

1 John 1:7

A couple months later John and I attended a "Marriage Enrichment
Weekend" at our church. As the weekend progressed we were
thrilled to find out that our love was deeper than a knowing in
mind and body love, or an emotional love (although these aspects
are certainly a part of our love), we experienced the love of total
acceptance. We *really liked* each other.

Sunday morning we met briefly with our sub-group before
joining the others in a circle in Fellowship Hall. There was a long,
low table covered to the floor with a crisp, white linen tablecloth.
The centerpiece was a tall, white, Christ's candle surrounded with
clusters of grapes. There were six silver trays spaced evenly
around the table with small loaves of broken bread on them. A
silver goblet stood beside each tray. We sang softly and prayed.
The Lord's presence and love were almost tangible.

John and I knelt beside the table as he placed the bread into
the fruit of the vine and then into my mouth saying, "This is the
blood and body of my Lord Jesus Christ." I did the same for him.
We hugged in silent prayer and praise. Our God is *so good.*

We had been looking at wide gold wedding bands for several
years, but thankfully we had not gotten around to buying them.

This was the perfect time for new rings. We bought them the week before the marriage enrichment seminar, and had arranged with David to renew our wedding vows on Sunday afternoon.

I bought a new red dress for the occasion. The red was symbolic of the Blood of Jesus. I knew that it was only through the Blood of Jesus that our marriage was saved and it was only through the Blood of Jesus that our marriage was going to stay saved.

Jesus had given us a totally new marriage and we wanted to dedicate it to Him, and to pledge ourselves to each other with believing hearts—hearts that knew Jesus Christ as Lord and Savior, hearts that were filled with His Holy Spirit, hearts that were experiencing the love of 1 Corinthians 13.

It was a simple ceremony, but somehow I felt that it was pleasing to the Lord. He likes simple things. He had been invited to be part of the ceremony and the marriage this time. He honored that invitation with His blessed presence. Bathed in His love we prayed. We repeated our vows. We cried, we hugged, and exchanged our rings in the presence of David, Louise and our Living God.

Like many couples today, we had lived up to our own criteria for a happy marriage, but were still miserable. That is because it was *our* criteria, not God's. We thought we had it all figured out, and could make it work by ourselves. But none of us have the power within ourselves to bring the dead back to life. Any marriage without Jesus is dead no matter how thoroughly we deceive ourselves.

In Romans 7:2 Paul tells us that death breaks the bond between husband and wife. Here he is speaking of a physical death in a husband-wife relationship. There are other kinds of death that can come to a marriage. There can be a death between their souls (mind, wills, emotions), and death between them spiritually. I am not saying that these "deaths" give freedom to either partner to find other mates, but certainly they lie at the root of why so many "happily married" people feel something is missing in their lives, which makes them vulnerable to the temptations of unfaithfulness.

Dead marriages are like spiritually dead people. They do not look any different, but what you see is what you get. The outward shell is all there is to them. They are like the unmarked graves in

Luke 11:44, men walk by them without knowing the decay that is there, and like the five foolish virgins of Matthew 25, everything appeared to be fine.

We keep our marriage lamps polished brightly on the outside while the inside is corroded with pride, greed, self-indulgence, and a host of other sinful emotions. Sheer pretense is invading our marriages, breaking down communication, building walls and pushing us in different directions. Jesus said, "And if a house is divided against itself, that house cannot stand" (Mark 3:25).

We have met many couples that were convinced they were happily married, but as time passed they found out the hard way that their marriages were not as stable as they thought. Time to love gets shoved aside for more important things like meetings (church as well as business), TV, hobbies, and a host of technological toys. The demands of life can eat us alive if we let them, until there is not only no time for love, but no love.

Jesus said, "Because you are lukewarm, and neither cold nor hot, I will vomit you out of My mouth" (Revelation 3:16). The lukewarm marriage is a thriving species, but Jesus has provided an alternative. We can build our marriages on Jesus, or we can watch them crumble. John and I had to go through quite a purifying process to get our marriage back on track, so I do not say it lightly, IT WAS WORTH IT!

The Parable of the Seed of Marriage
(My paraphrase)

A farmer was out sowing seeds of marriage in his field. As he scattered the seed across the ground some fell beside the path, and the birds came and ate it. And some fell on rocky soil where there was little depth of earth; the marriages sprang up quickly enough in the shallow soil, but the hot sun soon scorched them and they withered and died, for they had so little root.

Other seeds fell among thorns, and the thorns choked out the tender marriages. But some fell on good soil, and produced a crop that was thirty, sixty, and even a hundred times as much as he had planted.

Now there is an explanation of this story. The hard path represents the hearts of the couple that hears about God's plan for marriage and do not understand it; then satan comes and snatches away the marriage.

The shallow, rocky soil represents the hearts of the couple that hears about God's marriage plan and receives it with real joy. But they do not have much depth in their lives, and the marriage does not root very deeply, and after awhile when trouble comes, or persecution begins, their enthusiasm fades and they divorce.

The ground covered with thistles represents the couple that hears the message, but the cares of this life and their longing for money choke out God's Word. They give less and less time to marriage maintenance, and their relationship goes downhill.

The good ground represents the hearts of the couple who listen to the message, understand it, and go out to lead thirty, sixty, or even a hundred others into the Kingdom of total marriage, directed and empowered by God.

Chapter 14

PRESSING IN

Finally, my brethren, be strong in the Lord and the power of His might. Put on the whole armor of God, that you may be able to stand against the wiles of the devil. For we do not wrestle against flesh and blood, but against principalities, against powers, against rulers of the darkness of this age, against spiritual hosts of wickedness in the heavenly places. Therefore take up the whole armor of God, that you may be able to withstand in the evil day, and having done all, to stand.

Ephesians 6:10-13

Two years had passed when John came home from classes looking pale and nervous. I could feel the anxiety in his words. "You'll never guess who I saw today."

"Who?"

"Carol."

"Carol? What is she doing here?"

"I don't know. I was going down the stairs to my Greek class, and she was on her way up. She stepped out and cornered me with fury on her face, asking if I had sent her a Valentine's Day card. I told her no. It seems someone sent her a Valentine and signed it 'Love, John.' Her husband opened it and he's furious. It is not from me."

As John repeated the conversation I had a deep peace within, I *knew* that this was an attack from the enemy, and that John had not sent the card. I was so sure that I told him I was going to look for

71

Carol and offer to check the signature in order to assure her that it was not from him.

It was a couple weeks later that I finally caught a glimpse of her walking down a hallway at the college.

"Carol!" She turned around with a surprised look.

"I would like to talk to you for a few minutes."

"Sure."

"Let's go sit in the chapel."

We tripped through the small talk as we made our way to a quiet corner.

"I just wanted to tell you that I *know* that John did not send you that card, and I would be willing to check out the signature for your assurance."

"Oh that! I know that John did not send it. A few days after I talked to him a young girl down the street (whose name was Carol) came over and asked if I had received a card from someone named John. It turned out that her boyfriend, John, had sent her card to the wrong address.

That issue being behind us, I began to share all the beautiful things the Lord had been working out in our marriage. I expected her response to be the same, but unfortunately it was not. Her husband had left her several times during the previous two years. He had just returned again and they had started going through some marriage counseling. She had been keeping all this bottled up inside because she did not want to make her husband look bad to family, friends, or colleagues. She had no one to talk to.

My heart ached for her. When I asked if I could pray for her and her family she was stunned, but said yes. With my arm around her shoulders I began to pray as she began to cry. Carol kept saying over and over, "You are such a lady." I wanted to chuckle because I never thought of myself like that. Then I realized that when Jesus is being manifested in a woman's life she is seen as "such a lady."

"How can you be so forgiving and loving?" she asked. I filled her in on my bout with unforgiveness, and how I had learned the hard way that it can cripple a life if you let it take root. But a willingness to see people as Jesus sees them, a willingness to forgive sets our spirits free.

"You know, satan does not want us to forgive because that cuts down on his play room. He tries to keep our minds full of accusations, old sins and failings—all kinds of little darts that would prick our balloons." This is what is called spiritual warfare.

One of the main exercises in this battle is praise. I am thankful that I had a good solid praise teaching before this all happened. I knew to praise God, not *for* what was coming down, but to praise Him *in the midst of* what was happening. As painful as it was at times, Jesus was right there with us. It is essential that we praise Him in spite of the circumstances. When our minds are full of praise to the Lord there is no room for the negative attacks of the enemy. He just gets squeezed out. Praise releases God's power in our lives because He lives in the praises of His people (Psalm 22:3).

Another exercise in spiritual warfare is taking authority. I had a pressing problem with mental pictures regarding John's unfaithfulness. The girl had been my best friend. Satan kept popping scenes of them together into my mind. In 2 Corinthians 10:5 it tells us that we are to cast down our imaginations and bring every thought captive to the obedience of Christ. I kept speaking that over and over. "Jesus, I bring this thought captive to You. I rebuke it in the name of Jesus."

This was not a one-time confession. It was a daily, sometimes hourly confession. The mental torment would leave, but then it would come back. Colossians 3:2 says, "Set your mind on things above, and not on things on the earth." We have to keep watch over our thoughts at all times. Think about what you are thinking about. Isaiah says of God, "You will keep him in perfect peace, whose mind is stayed on You" (Isaiah 26:3).

My prayer language was another key weapon in my spiritual warfare. It did what God created it to do. It strengthened me, drew me closer to Him, and it raised me above the problem.

One other thing that I shared with Carol was the importance of releasing her husband to God. She did not have him physically bound up, but her critical, worrisome thoughts and emotions toward him were strong invisible cords that bound him. The Lord had taught me to release John each morning. I would picture myself lifting him up to Jesus, and taking my hands off. When I first did this, John came to me saying that he felt a new freedom, and that there was something different about me.

Jesus says that whatever we bind on earth shall be bound in heaven, and whatever we loose on earth shall be loosed in heaven (Matthew 18:18). Jesus said this in context of Matthew 18: 15-35, which teaches about the power we have in forgiveness!

Chapter 15

A CLEAR CONSCIENCE

Submit to God. Resist the devil and he will flee from you.
James 4:7

The Lord had clearly directed us to an Institute of Basic Youth Conflicts seminar in June of 1978. My heart was prepared and eager to receive further direction for my life. When Mr. Gothard began quoting 1 Timothy 1:18-19 I knew this was a key verse for me. ". . . wage the good warfare, having faith and a good conscience . . ."

He said a clear conscience is a necessity for being effective in spiritual warfare—it is a *must*. He told us to envision a picture frame, and to ask the Holy Spirit to place within that frame the faces of those people from whom we needed to ask forgiveness.

Much to my surprise my own face was the first to appear. The Lord began to speak to my heart of the need to forgive myself for our premarital relationship. I knew that God had forgiven me. I had forgiven John, but I had never forgiven myself. Even when God showed me this, after thirteen years of marriage it was still hard to confront. It took hours of tears and discussion with John before coming to the place where I was willing to forgive myself. The obedience resulted in the instant release of a haunting, heavy weight that had been hanging on my heart.

There were several other faces that came into focus in my picture frame over the next twenty-four hours. One in particular profoundly influenced my life. Diane had been my best friend, the one with whom John had been unfaithful. I was startled to see her face. I cried out to God, "What do I need to ask *her* forgiveness?" The still small voice was clear, "Self-righteousness and a prideful attitude toward her."

We had not planned on taking any side trips, but the Holy Spirit clearly indicated that we needed to make one. I was intensely apprehensive about seeing Diane again. I had no idea of how either of us was going to receive the other. We had not seen each other in years. I called ahead and she sounded eager to see us. When we arrived at her home she greeted me with open arms, and graciously invited us in as if nothing had ever happened. I was there to do business, so I did not let any time fly under my feet. I immediately explained why I was there.

I told her about the picture frame, and asked her to forgive me for the self-righteousness and pride I had exhibited when I was supposedly her friend. Diane burst out in heart-wrenching tears. "Forgive *you*? *I'm* the one who needs to ask forgiveness. I'm *so sorry.*" I put my arms around her, patted her head and told her it was all right. I had forgiven her long ago.

When I think of my time with her I equate it with times I have spent with my children when they have been hurt and have come to me. I would love them and hold them close, letting them cry on my shoulder. Jesus loved Diane through me that day. I knew it was not Kathy Hendershot—it was Jesus Christ.

It tore me up to see her hurting. She had no one to talk to. She had confessed to her husband years before, however, his pain stood between them. Diane had grown up in an evangelical church that ministered salvation, but not the edification and teaching on spiritual warfare needed to deal with everyday life. She carried her guilt and shame all alone, not knowing the promises of forgiveness that were hers.

For three hours the Holy Spirit ministered to her, helping her to accept the forgiveness that was bought for her on the cross— after all that is the reason Jesus came. He did not come for a pure and holy people, He came for a people who were sick, sinful, and in need of a Savior—a people He could make pure and holy. He tells us, "If we confess our sins, He is faithful and just to forgive us our sins and to cleanse us from all unrighteousness" (1 John 1:9). If we do not accept His forgiveness and cleansing then Jesus died for us in vain.

Later John told me that when we first started talking he thought he should leave the room, but he was held captive as he watched the way Jesus was ministering to her. Something exciting was taking place. He sat as quiet as the proverbial mouse in the corner. After a few hours of ministry, the message finally soaked in. I wrote out a page of scripture verses on forgiveness for her to meditate on. John saw an ominous cloud of darkness move from over her head as Jesus ministered to her that day.

I had forgiven Diane almost immediately (about 20%). Through praying for her over the years, my forgiveness grew to about 80%. But that day I forgave her 100%, and never had trouble with mental pictures again. My memory of Diane is as a precious sister in the Lord, a sinner saved by grace, just like me.

The lesson of handling the crisis of life according to God's Word and God's Spirit is actually coping with life as it really is, not as it seems to be. When this takes place we are no longer ruled by circumstances, we overcome them.

PART III

HEALING and WALKING

Chapter 16

HEALING IS AVAILABLE

And Jesus went about all Galilee, teaching in their synagogues, preaching the gospel of the kingdom, and healing all kinds of sickness and all kinds of disease among the people. Then His fame went throughout all Syria; and they brought to Him all their sick people who were afflicted with various diseases and torments, and those who were demon-possessed, epileptics, and paralytics; and He healed them.

Matthew 4:23–24

Realizing that John's graduation was hastily approaching and that we would no longer have any kind of insurance, we sagaciously stampeded to the Hunter Foundation. This was a fine medical organization that established a moderate monthly fee for its members according to their income, and henceforth provided all medical services, including medicine, without charge. It was a great comfort to know that we would never encounter exorbitant medical bills—a little too much comfort. The Lord whispered into my heart that I was depositing my trust in this organization instead of Him.

We abandoned this common form of security in 1978 and only incurred one medical bill during those early years of our obedience walk. No, we are not "lucky." The Psalmist says,

> Bless the Lord, O my soul, and forget not all His benefits: Who forgives all your iniquities, Who heals all your diseases, Who redeems your life from destruction, Who crowns you with loving kindness and tender mercies, Who satisfies your mouth with good things, so that your youth is renewed like the eagles (Psalm 103:2–3).

I am not implying that everyone reading these words should cancel their health insurance. The Lord spoke to us directly on this matter, and we were obliged to obey. We were also drowsily awakening to the fact that God was doing a unique work in our lives.

One day after school Christi slammed the car door on her fingers. My immediate response to her blood-curdling cry was to jump out of the car and jerk the back door open. Its metal jaws had smashed her little fingers into the width of a dime. I am not sure what my response would have been under ordinary circumstances, but this was during a season when I was teaching on the power of the blood of Jesus at the Lexington Bible Institute. My spirit was so full of the Word of God from diligent study and teaching this series that I lost no time in authoritatively rebuking the enemy's plan to harm my child, and appropriating the blood of Jesus upon her hand. I rushed her into the school kitchen and applied ice as I continued to pray for her. The pain subsided and we left for home.

Our original plan was to stop at the mall and pick out some material she needed for a class project, but *under the circumstances* I felt we should wait for another day. "Oh, no," Christi pleaded, "please let's do it today." "Are you sure you feel up to it?" I asked. "Yes. I'm fine," she replied.

After a successful shopping expedition we headed home to relay the day's activities to John—especially the details of Christi's traumatic trial. But when she stuck her hand out to show him her hurt fingers there was absolutely nothing to show—no swelling, no discoloration, and no pain—nothing. Christi giggled and ran off to practice her piano lesson.

Another time Kevin was spending the night with a friend. The friend's mother called us early the next morning and said that he had been up all night throwing up, had a fever and her husband was taking him to the emergency room. At this time I was studying the power of praising God in everything—not *for* everything, but *in the midst* of everything. When I hung up the phone I heard the Holy Spirit's whisper in my spirit, "You have a choice: panic or praise." I chose to praise. I started praying in my prayer language and singing praise choruses for the half-hour trip to Central Baptist Hospital and never stopped until hours later when the crisis had passed.

When I arrived at the hospital the nurses were prepping Kevin for surgery to take out his appendix. Kevin was doubled over on the examination table, having just had x-rays taken. He was as white as the proverbial sheet, almost unconscious and groaning with every breath. I put my hands on his head while I kept softly singing and praising God. About an hour later they began a final exam before the intended operation. Much to their surprise his blood count was returning to normal as well as his temperature. They never operated on Kevin, and to this day he still has his appendix.

The doctors insisted that Kevin stay overnight for observation, but first thing the next morning we checked in with the nurse concerning taking him home. She said that he still had a slight temperature and they would not release him with a temperature. John and I found a quiet corner to join together in prayer. Within a half-hour he was checked again—no fever. We took our son home.

A few years later, doctors told me I needed two operations, but since we did not have medical insurance I declined. I had no choice but to trust God for my healing, and He healed me.

My body had developed a goiter when I was about twelve years old, causing my Adam's Apple to appear quite pronounced. I attended a Vickie Jamison healing service when I was in my fifties, received a brief prayer, and Jesus dissolved that goiter completely.

• • • • •

These years continued to be life changing in the area of inner healing as well. It was a matter of allowing Jesus to tenderly walk me back in time to face corrosive childhood memories, and appropriate His healing work. Yes, we had begun in David's office several years earlier, and yes, my responsibility to forgive and to ask for forgiveness played a major role, but by His grace every nook and cranny of my soul was in a renewal process.

Psychologist tell us that only 10% of our thinking is conscious, leaving 90% of our thoughts floating around seemingly unaccounted for in our subconscious. The problem is that painful memories that we block out hold a strong influence over us, and color the way we act, think, and respond. Inner healing is *not* a process of digging up garbage, it is a matter of getting rid of garbage—a decidedly distinct difference. It is unhealthy to be so intricately introspective that we are constantly thinking about ourselves, but until our souls (minds, wills, and emotions) are healed, our base of operation is going to be self. We cannot heal a wound by saying it is not there. If our pasts are not healed then we are prisoners of them, and we will not be free to become all that God intended us to be.

Research has revealed that when an event takes place we store the facts and feelings in our minds and emotions. When Jesus heals a hurtful memory the facts remain the same, but the way we feel about them changes. For me inner healing was predominantly a five-year process, coming at it from various perspectives. The Holy Spirit did the work, but I had to be willing to let Him move freely within me. He is a gentleman. He will not force us to do anything. His timing is perfect, the work is personalized, and the reality of Jesus Christ and His healing power is transforming.

This is not something that just happened. I sought inner healing with all my being, desperately desiring to love God with all my heart, and soul, and strength, and my mind, but sensing that childhood hurts were steeled away in part of my heart. Things that are buried alive cause a stink, and keep us from total surrender. I would need help in identifying my personal skunks and bringing them to the cross.

At times it felt that I was living in an never-ending self-focused pit, but the thing that kept me moving on in the healing process was heartfelt burden to free my children from the consequences of damaged relationships. I could see how my attitudes, pain, judgments, and reactions were affecting their lives. Jesus said, "For their sakes I sanctify Myself, that they also may be sanctified by the truth." Of course He had no sin, but when I read those words in John 17:19, they came alive to me. It was as though the Holy Spirit was saying to me that if I cooperated and allowed Him to do a healing work in my mind, my will, and my emotions it would be a blessing for my children. The motivation to be obedient to the promptings of the Holy Spirit, and to do a work that would have eternal ramifications for my children kept me anchored to the inner healing process.

One of the first areas where the Holy Spirit shed His light came to my attention during a class on the Christian Education. We were given an exercise that would help us understand a person's background by having them draw a picture of their childhood dinner table—showing where various family members sat, what they looked like, and sharing interactions or conversations that may have taken place. We broke up into small groups and shared our individual depictions.

I was the only one in my picture. I was an only child. My father worked nights and he and my mother would eat dinner before he went to work at three in the afternoon, while I was still in school. He would already be gone when I got home. I would be in bed when he returned from work, and up and out to school before he arose in the morning, so we would go weeks at a time without seeing each other. He was basically an absentee father because he worked this shift seven days a week for years.

This realization made me sad until the picture in my mind sharpened to the detail of the design on the table. It was an old Formica table with chrome stripes around the edge, and a pattern of red and gray fish around the entire perimeter. Each form of the fish was a simple stick-like drawing that we frequently see representing Ichthus—the ancient symbol for Jesus—I just *thought* I was all alone back then, but *Jesus was there.* What a powerful revelation! No words can describe the flood of love from the Father that filled my little-girl heart. The tears of joy cleansed a deep pit of loneliness and Jesus filled it with His healing presence.

My attention was now focused on my relationship or lack thereof, with my father. I had no recollection of either of us verbally expressing our love for one another, although there was a mindset that of course we loved each other. John and I were expecting an immanent visit from my parents when it became clear to me that the Lord was asking me to make a verbal expression of my love for my dad. I practiced several scenarios for this to take place, none of which materialized.

My parents had been in our home a couple days when Daddy had the bright idea that he, my children, and I would have a picnic on the college campus. The fact that he came up with this proposal was in itself a shock. I do not remember why my mother and John were not in on this unique experience, but I do remember sitting on the steps of Hughes Auditorium enjoying the picnic fare, while thinking "I can't believe I am sitting here having a picnic with *my father*."

As the weekend was winding down I was winding up into a ball of nerves. Time was running out and I had not made my earthshaking proclamation yet! At breakfast on Sunday morning somehow I found myself alone with my dad at the kitchen table (which was a miracle in itself—and to this day I do not know how the other five family members disappeared). With panic flowing through my veins I reached over and placed my right hand upon his left hand, which was in a resting position on the table. With my eyes diverted to the tabletop I softly exhaled, "Daddy I love you." With his eyes equally diverted, he responded, "I love you too, sweetheart." Nothing more was said, but my heart was at ease and filled with a refreshing that satisfied a little girl's hungering to hear her father's voice confirm his love for her.

When I graduated from college a couple years later I had the joy of watching my father and my youngest child running around taking pictures of me as I walked in the processional. It would have been tempting to be embarrassed at all the attention, but it turned out to be such an edifying experience to see my father so excited and proud of me. Several weeks later when we were helping my parents clean out their attic, Mom and I sorted out some old pictures and I confiscated several from my early childhood. A few days after returning home the pictures from my graduation were developed.

As I studied these current pictures of me with my dad, and then focused on the old pictures of me with my dad, the Lord touched my heart with His love and compassion. I was able to receive my father's love afresh, both for the present and the past. I stared at that man lovingly looking into my bassinet with the same love and pride I saw on his face in my graduation pictures. My father did love me from the very beginning of my life. I just did not know it. These were once more, holy moments of healing revelation.

Several months later John and I attended a Faith At Work Conference that was being led by Francis and Judith MacNutt. Things were moving along rather smoothly until the last day. The previous evening Judith had prayed that the Holy Spirit would bring to our consciousness anything that was hidden in our souls that needed to be healed. That night I had a dream and woke up sobbing. The scene was a vivid memory from my childhood that had taken place on several occasions. I saw my enraged mother repeatedly screaming at me, "I could kill you! I could kill you!" In the dream she was standing in front of me holding a gun aimed straight at me. The fear and sense of rejection were paralyzing.

I could not control my crying. As best I could I gulped the sobs back, washed my face and went to breakfast, but I could not eat. I returned to my room with an urgency to find privacy for the release of the erupting emotions. Memories of my father's disappointment in my never accomplishing the "star-status" of a Mouseketeer, a Lennon Sister, or Miss America flooded my overtaxed emotions with an added sting. There was no one with me in that room, but I knew that God was reaching down to me, healing and comforting me as only He could—pulling out the painful barbs, while at the same time applying the Balm of Gilead. After settling myself, I once more gathered the strength to venture over to the morning session. I sat in the last seat on the back row so as not to disturb anyone or draw attention to myself. That seemed like it would be a safe place to hide out when it came time for ministry.

The tears gushed throughout the praise and prayer time, but remained more muffled during the teaching. As Francis and Judith prepared to pray for people, they gave instruction that they would be ushering us to the front by rows in order for them to lay hands on us and anoint us with oil. They were starting with the back row! I dragged my weary well-watered body to the front and received another measure of healing—another layer of my onionskin had been peeled off.

After lunch we picked up our son, who had been attending the same conference, but had been bunking with the youth in a separate area of the park. When I saw him I immediately blurted out, "I am so ashamed of you!" because he still had on the clothes he had worn to the conference *three days before.* But as I heard myself utter those words I realized that that was not true—it was what I call a Holy Spirit setup. Those were words that my mother had used to humiliate me. I realized that the shame that I had been carrying all those years was being exposed and healed as the Holy Spirit ministered to me in that moment, and allowed me to ask my son's forgiveness and to express my love for him just as he is. It was a cleansing work of God from the shame that my mother had put on me, and I had received.

I cried most of the four-hour trip home as another phrase that my mother "named" me with came back to my memory—"Her Royal Highass." The cleansing continued to be released through more tears, and more tears. Of course, as we have already covered, the willingness to forgive was in play throughout this whole ordeal. This is **not** a blame game. Hurting people hurt people, and my mother was a hurting person (more of her story later). I expose these now-healed wounds for the benefit of others—in order that they may know that there is total healing available for deep, long-hidden hurts no matter what the particulars of their situation may look like. Jesus is the healer of our souls as well as our bodies.

In John 8:32 it says that you will know the truth and the truth will set you free. That is what Jesus has done in my life. He has shown me truth—the real me. In John 1:34 John the Baptist says, "I have seen, and my testimony is that this is the Son of God." I echo his testimony today. We cannot be whole people without all our pieces. Jesus takes broken pieces and heals, mends, and restores. That is what this book is all about. It is an example, not of perfection, but of the process of transformation, of being made whole by trusting and obeying Him one step at a time. Jesus said, "Without Me, you can do nothing (John 15:5). But He also said that *with Him all* things are possible (Mark 10:27).

There is a difference between being cleansed, and being made whole. If there is a chip out of your good china plate you can still wash it and make it clean, but you cannot replace the missing chip. If we think of our lives as china plates we can see that Jesus cannot only clean us up, He can replace the chips and make us whole.

Jesus filled me with Himself. Then He gently took me by the hand and led me to the broken pieces of my life. One by one we gathered them up and He grafted them back into place. It was painful but I was not alone. He never left me, and none of the pieces were lost.

> Humpty Dumpty sat on a wall.
> Humpty Dumpty had a great fall.
> Humpty Dumpty shouted, "Amen!
> God can put me together again."
> (Marjorie Decker, *The Christian Mother Goose)*

Chapter 17

STEPPING OUT

Trust in the Lord with all your heart, and lean not to your own understanding; in all your ways acknowledge Him, and He shall direct your paths.

Proverbs 3:5–6

By the time that John graduated from Asbury we had totally deflated our financial cushion. The rent that June was paid via generous graduation gifts. He had vigorously volunteered at Gospel Graphics on a full-time basis the previous summer, and believed that he was to continue in this obedience ministry upon graduation. (We preferred to call it an obedience ministry, rather than a faith ministry, because we did not consider ourselves to be people of great faith. We were just trying to be obedient to what we believed the Lord was telling us to do, trusting Him alone to provide the support needed to get the job done). The ensuing fourteen years were years of testing and trials in learning to trust God for our *daily* bread. In the process we acquired a storehouse of sustaining verifications that *He* is faithful.

One brisk, fall evening our challenging circumstances looked ominous. No food, no money—John and I questioningly searched each other's face when he walked through the door at dinnertime. Each was hoping that the other one had some good news. We meandered into our tiny kitchen and stared at the empty cupboards, trying to pool our culinary talents together and make something out of nothing (which has been accomplished on occasion). Suddenly we heard a gentle tapping on the front door. I pulled back the curtain to view one of our dear friends juggling several boxes of food. The church where she and her husband were serving as student-pastors had given them an old fashioned "pounding." Each person brought a pound of flour, or a pound of butter, a pound of this, or a pound of that. Ernie and Sandy had way more than they could use or shelve in their equally tiny college-housing kitchen, so they wondered if they could share with us. The Holy Spirit reminded me of the Scripture, "I have been young and now am old; yet have I not seen the righteous forsaken, nor his seed begging bread" (Psalm 37:25).

Our Christmas season that year was the pits. This was the first time we could not buy our children Christmas presents—and we were treeless. We had planned on being at my parent's home on Christmas Day, and they would have a tree, but it did not seem like the Christmas season without one in our home. Much to my surprise the kids did not even care. As my self-pity eased away the Lord showed me that had I been holding onto a false value in sentimental tradition, and these "things" were just not important.

Determined to make the best of the situation, I hauled out my sewing machine and fashioned skirts and vests for the girls, and a long nightshirt for Kevin (which was a hilarious hit)! My eyes certainly were focused on Jesus by the time that Christmas Day dawned that year. He *is* all I need.

* * * * *

Our lifestyle soothingly settled into a welcomed routine that next year. Gospel Graphics was prospering and we were receiving regular financial provision from His hand, when faint little nudges began jostling our spirits. It was time to press on. The gentle wind of the Spirit was wistfully whistling, "Come on. Naptime is over. We've got work to do."

In the natural we were not eager to "forsake all" again, but we were not willing to coast into spiritual sluggishness either. We knew that God was explicitly exhorting John to leave Gospel Graphics and undertake another step of obedience. Every night after dinner John and I burdensomely walked the block and cried together as the Lord confirmed His will in our hearts.

John had devotedly served this ministry for three years. He poured his life into it, therefore the pain he felt was comparable to leaving a part of himself. Months down the road the Lord was still confirming that this was His will. The following prophecy was given through Red and Peggy Stanley, who were seasoned servants in prophetic ministry, on October 17, 1980. They had no clue in the natural as to what the Lord was speaking to our hearts.

> John, you've gone through much. You've yielded to the Lord in many things, and many times you have been unsung and unheralded, but the Lord is going to lift you up into a new place because He has heard the cry of your heart. I don't know anything, but I saw you crying in your heart. He is going to lift you into a new place. I wish I could tell you what it is, but I don't know.
>
> You and your wife together have been climbing some mountains and you know what the scripture says, 'speak to the mountains and they will be cast into the sea.' But there are some mountains we have to climb. You are making a way for some people that have to climb them because you're leaving spikes so that somebody can come up behind you.
>
> The Lord's blessing is upon you. He's seen and He's stored up. Be encouraged. You know what I am saying. The Lord knows and you know, and His hand is stretched forth to bless you. Both of you—be encouraged. Be strengthened.

John's vision was to minister to ministers and ministries, to serve and support them in any way he could. His aspiration was to provide office space, secretarial help, legal help, computer services, counseling, newsletters, printing, whatever would be needed, and all at minimum or no charge according to the budgets of the ministries involved. He would call this new endeavor Christian Ministries, Inc. (CMI).

When the pastor of Woodland Avenue Baptist Church considered John's vision, he offered a huge, old, 6000 square foot house that the church owned. John was given permission to use the old house as long as he wanted to, for whatever he wanted to do with it.

173 Woodland Avenue must have been quite a showplace in its time (early 1900s), but through the years it had drastically

deteriorated from lack of use. John was ecstatic over his new "offices" as if they were executive suites in a presidential palace. Frankly, I was not favorably impressed, and did not covet any part of fixing up this monstrous nightmare. But as usual, God had other plans.

On January 1, 1981 I was sweeping sooty floors and cleaning out the ash-filled fireplaces between mad dashes to the heat vent to thaw out. All-the-while wrestling with a dreaded knowing in my spirit that I was going to have an active role in this house of God's.

Before the day was over John had discovered a thick bolt of shell colored satin amongst the residue of the previous inhabitants. It happened to be the exact shade he had envisioned for the draperies that would eventually adorn the nine humongous (indicative of huge and monstrous) windows in the front rooms. I listlessly measured the window frames and calculated that we would need fifty-two yards of material for the project. Later measurements confirmed there were fifty-two yards of satin on that bolt. Once again I experienced a dreaded knowing in my spirit that I was going to be the designated seamstress.

I had never made a drape in my life, did not know how, and did want to know how! I diligently questioned my friends, "Do you know how to make drapes?" Eventually Joan Tighe offered some helpful hints and some labor. Begrudgingly I began to cut, pin, and stitch. With Joan's encouragement, direction and hemming we completed the unpopular project within a week. After several more weeks of cleaning and painting at Christian Ministries our hearty efforts seemed to have accomplished only a dent of difference until we hung the drapes. Then even my perfectionistic pessimism was silenced. We were making progress.

An effusion of prophecy came forth from several sources that God had ordained Christian Ministries to be a storehouse. Again this was confirmation to what God had already spoken to our hearts. People would be coming from all over, and God would meet their needs here. We were also believing that He would provide opportunities for us to reach out in several unconventional ways.

With this in mind, John was determined to pay for his own plane ticket (about $500) to Winnipeg, Manitoba. He had been asked to do some troubleshooting for Trinity Television in Canada.

He had made arrangements well in advance, but the finances were not in hand. The ticket on John's desk was stamped, "Void if not paid within ten days." Ten days had passed weeks ago.

It was a cold, windy and rainy Monday morning in May. I walked into the office and found John with his soul reflecting the dismal day's weather condition. He was all dressed up. His bags were packed ready to meet the 11 a.m. flight, but no money—only a void ticket in hand. He prostrated himself on the long, low table he called his desk, and called out to God. "Here I am" he dramatized, "a living sacrifice. What do you want me to do?"

Ninety-five percent of the time, when one of us is spiritually low the other is high. In accordance with the John-Kathy law, my response was laughter. I composed myself enough to offer a candid little prayer on the heels of which I daringly questioned, "Well you're going out to the airport aren't you?" He looked at me with one of those "Have you lost your mind?" looks. "Why should I go out to the airport?"

"To take the ticket back." I mischievously smiled as if I knew something was about to happen.

John's countenance lifted instantly. "Right. Let's go!"

John commandingly maneuvered our station wagon into the airport parking lot at 10:40. I was in no rush—we were not going anywhere. John jumped out, jerked the backdoor open and proceeded to unload his luggage. He looked up and asked me matter-of-factly, "Will you carry my suit bag?"

"I thought you were just going to return the ticket." Now my side of the seesaw was dragging in unbelief, and he was being the great saint of faith and power!

As we pompously paraded into that lobby I had a mental picture of two children playing "airport." I posed in a seat beside the luggage as if I was supposed to be there. John stood surveying the crowd. I am not sure what we were expecting—maybe someone to walk up to us and hand us the money for the ticket.

At 10:50 John announced, "If we're going to make a move we'd better do it now." We nonchalantly armed ourselves with his luggage and headed to the ticket counter. Immediately the man behind the counter looked up and said, "I need to check-in your baggage."

"But we're not sure this ticket is paid for—could you check it out? John persisted, anticipating that someone may have sent the money without our knowledge.

"I'll have to call Cincinnati." He proceeded to call, then routinely informed us that, "No. The ticket has not been financed. I've *got* to check your baggage and get you on that plane," he insistently repeated.

"But how can you check his baggage if his ticket has not been paid for?" I asked.

"Oh, we have these big guys that go around knocking on doors when people don't pay up," he seemed to jest.

We could not believe it. They were actually going to let him board a plane with an invalid ticket!

We juggled back and forth with "What do you think?"

"Well, I don't know. What do you think?"

Finally I ventured, "Well the Lord didn't close the door. You *can* get on the plane."

"Right. Let's go!"

It amazes me still as I look back that we were not frantically running to the plane. It was 11:05.

John was carrying a case of videotapes, which could not be passed through the x-ray machine so we had to open and close twenty cases for the guards to check. After this delay we were still moving in slow motion as if we had all the time in the world.

As we approached the gate the attendant, while dutifully collecting and stamping the tickets, was shaking his head with a disgusted look on his face. "Somebody sure wants you on that plane. I've been held up on the phone —that flight should have taken off fifteen minutes ago!"

John and I were about to pop! He *briskly* boarded the plane. They latched the door and took off.

We know now why the enemy did not want John on that plane. He was able to help Trinity deal with some major bottlenecks in their organization. He was a guest on their T. V. program for three days. People accepted Jesus as their Savior. Marriages were healed, and the Lord ministered to a countless number of people as he shared his testimony.

John did not tell his hosts in Canada the details of his trip, but while attending a business meeting with them later that week, a man stood up and unexpectedly announced that the board had decided to pay for John's flight!

Chapter 18

MY HIDING PLACE

You are a hiding place for me; You, Lord, preserve me from
trouble, You surround me with songs and shouts of deliverance.
Selah [pause and calmly think of that]!

Psalm 32:7 (Amplified)

After my graduation from Asbury College we rented a house in
Nicholasville for a year. Our lease was to be up at the end of May,
and we believed we were to relocate to Lexington somewhere in
the vicinity of CMI. We proceeded to pack up and launch out to
Lexington. As the date for our departure drew near it became clear
that we would be temporarily camping out at the Christian
Ministries building.

You already have a vivid description of my sentiments
concerning this historical habitat being utilized for offices, so you
can imagine how overjoyed I was regarding the prospect of living
there. This antiquated dwelling had no kitchen, no tub or shower,
and no washer or dryer hookups. Our ten-gallon hot water heater
was on the blink as well. To make our little haven even more
alluring, there was an eight-piece Christian band that practiced
faithfully on the second floor. This was not my idea of twentieth
century living.

The neighborhood was two blocks from the University of
Kentucky, and provided enough local color to keep my prayer line
jammed 24/7! John spent two or three nights a week at Lynn Blue

Print that summer, printing newsletters for various missionaries until three or four o'clock in the morning leaving me as the senior member of the night watch brigade. My eyes popped open and my nerves jumped through my skin at every little click or thud until he returned home.

Bob and Marcy Gosselin brought their son up to summer school and spent a couple nights with us in our exotic quarters. Bob wisely wheeled Rob's new ten-speed bicycle into the house that first night. In the morning while we were preparing for a drive to Wilmore, he mounted the classy bike onto the back of his car, came back in for another suitcase, and by the time he returned to the car the bike was gone.

We were sickened by their loss, but even more aware of what went on in this neighborhood. Knowing that we were being spied upon left me feeling extremely vulnerable. Eventually I grew out of my initial fears, but remained cautious, always making sure that the children did not go out alone. We committed their safety to the Lord. We knew that His angels were a greater protection than we could ever be, and that God did not want us living in fear. 2 Timothy 1:7 says, "For God has not given us the spirit of fear, but of power and of love and of a sound mind." "The horse is prepared for the day of battle, but deliverance is of the Lord" (Proverbs 21:31). "For I know whom I have believed, and am persuaded that he is able to keep that *which I have committed unto him until* that day" (2 Timothy 1:12).

There were not many rooms in livable condition so John and I slept on the couch, which folded out into a bed, and taped large garbage bags across those humongous windows every night. Of course the garbage bags had to be removed at a decent hour—this was an office during the day. I was cornered on a couple occasions into chatting with visitors before the bedroom was disassembled as if lying there clutching the covers up under my chin were a normal everyday occurrence.

The children were stacked into one little room that looked like the ceiling was going to cave in if anyone sneezed. John assured us that it was safe, but in the winter (yes, we were still there in the winter), it was a little drafty so John taped some wrapping paper over the more breezy places. When the wind blew, the paper would rattle rhythmically. Christi would giggle and tell us it was the Tidy Bowl man up there.

The Lord blessed us with many dear, dear friends who became like family to us. Upon moving into Christian Ministries we were given keys to a number of homes in order to do laundry, take baths and showers as we wished. We did a lot of house sitting for people that summer.

Many families invited us to "dinner and showers." One couple had us over to dinner sixteen times in our first month at Christian Ministries, and invited us many more evenings, but we declined, believing that they deserved a break. Their support extended to the point that when they went on vacation they left us enough money for two weeks of groceries. They had caught a vision of what we were trying to do, and wanted to help us do it. A priceless relationship was built between our families, as we became a part of each other's lives.

Another single friend loved having us over for baths and showers. She worked all day and usually came home to an empty apartment. There again the Lord established a special relationship. When her heat went out the following winter she felt free to come and stay with us for a week.

Things started looking up in August. We were able to buy some copper pipe, and get a water heater hooked up in the basement. We had a spigot for a shower, and about two feet down the wall had two more spigots for a sink. The church next door had an old utility tub they were not using that the men installed next to our shower spigot (with a shower curtain strung between the two).

With only a ten-gallon hot water heater we often had to decide if we were going to do the dishes, or if someone was going to get a shower. When I did opt to do dishes the only drainage for the water was a plug that let the water straight down to the floor that slanted to a drainage pipe. John built me a wooden platform to keep my feet dry.

A friend found a stove in an old trailer, and another friend fixed it up for us. The electricians from Woodland Avenue Baptist Church wired the basement for the stove, as well as for my washer and dryer. This brought temporary relief until the neighbors began noticing the soapy water flowing from our house down to Central Avenue (the drain was not connected to the sewer properly). It was back to lugging our laundry elsewhere, but relationships were being built and God majors in relationships.

One Saturday afternoon I was lying on the couch feeling sorry for myself because we did not have any food, when I heard someone pounding on the back door. The man announced he had a donation for Christian Ministries. He asked if we would help unload it. I pictured a baby elephant or some such joke, but as I peeked into his van I discovered wall-to-wall bags of groceries, well over $200 worth.

Our kids played grocery store all afternoon as they stacked and re-stacked the shelves with cans of food. It was a heartfelt blessing to witness the impact that God's faithfulness had upon our children. Yes, a man gave of his resources, and we were truly thankful for him, but he was acting out of obedience to what God had laid on his heart.

The hardest area for me to deal with at Christian Ministries was the lack of privacy. The night before we moved in some friends had us to dinner. It was after ten o'clock when we pulled into the driveway and saw the house all lit up and pulsating with music. The screenless windows on the second floor were wide open loosing a beat that actually was vibrating the whole house.

When we rounded into the carport and beheld the back door, which was also invitingly open to whosoever will, I wanted to scream. Strange people were rambling in and out. We had left Christi's puppy on the back porch because we had not had time to train her—she was not housebroken. "Cuddles" was nowhere to be seen.

I stalked up the stairs in a rage. The trombone player was doing his thing in the hallway. "Have you seen our puppy?" "Yeah. I think I saw her on the other side of the glass doors with the other dog." My heart sank. Not because she was not housebroken, but because we had locked *our* section off, and if somebody put her in *our* section they must have found a way in— nothing was secure!

The puppy was fine. As I set about making up the beds the Lord began gently stroking my soul. "Calm down. Calm down. This is *My* house. Be thankful that these are Christian boys." I knew he was right. How possessive I had become over this old place. Later on one of the boys came to apologize. He explained that when he came in with his arms full of equipment the puppy had run out ahead of him and jumped through a lower frame in the French door where the pane was missing. Because of the Lord's chastening I could say, "No problem. Everything is fine."

The initial battle with the band was over, but each member had a key to the house, and they were in and out practicing at will. One night we were in bed at 10:30 p.m., and one of them walked in with his girlfriend. Over and over I had to surrender to sharing God's provision when it was not comfortable or easy. When I finally released them to the Lord, John gave them notice that they would have to leave because he was ready to start remodeling the second floor.

I wish historical accounts would prove to be a testimony of how graciously I accepted all this—how I allowed the Lord to lift me above it all, but the truth is I kicked most of the way. My will was set to endure, but I selfishly murmured and complained. It was through this walk of *external* obedience that I observed my *internal* disobedience—character flaws that I may never have dealt with otherwise, self-pity being a major one. The exciting thing about Jesus is that when He shows us our sin, then we can repent and He forgives us and cleans us up. Eventually we were able to set up some bedrooms, put in drop ceilings, and hang more curtains in this dwelling place that was to be called home for another two years.

Chapter 19

PERSONAL CARE

And my God shall supply all your need according to His riches in glory by Christ Jesus.

Philippians 4:19

God's faithfulness is the greatest reality of life. He is who He says He is, and He does what He says He will do. He has proven Himself over and over again. His name is *Jehovah-Jireh*, our provider. The following paragraphs contain a brief sampling of His phenomenal personal care for us during this season of our walk.

Christmas was just around the corner when a friend came by the office and urgently requested the use of our station wagon for an hour. He secretively mumbled something about picking up an item that would roll around too much in his van. His vague explanation sounded a little strange, but John said, "Sure."

An hour later her returned, and without any mention of his mysterious excursion handed us gift certificates for four haircuts and one permanent. His unconventional manner tickled us as much as his unconventional gift. Later that afternoon I bounced into the car to run an errand, and noticed the gas tank registered FULL. That is what our friend could not pick up with his own car!

The following Sunday this same family had us to dinner. We were about to leave when the husband asked John to stop by the Jaycee's office and pick up a package for him. He gave John $20 and said they would give him a green receipt. It was our Christmas tree!

That week another couple who generously and regularly supported Christian Ministries, and always made sure we had tickets for various church functions, came to volunteer for a whole day and brought a crock pot of chili and some homemade cupcakes for lunch.

The Lord meticulously arranged for both of us to attend the National Religious Broadcasters Convention in Washington DC that February. Trinity Television in Canada financed a booth in the exhibit hall. Our friend, John Hicks had recently taken a position as director of a retirement center in downtown DC and graciously invited us to be his guests. His wife, Donna, was maintaining their home in Lexington until it was sold and offered to keep all three of our children for the week.

We had enough capital to manage gas and one meal a day. My heart is burdened for people with marital and family problems so I naturally desired to attend the workshops on "Reaching the Family," but I was not registered, and the registration cost was over $100. John straightforwardly walked up to the registration desk and simply asked if his wife could have an exhibitor's badge. The lady typed one up and handed it to him, no questions asked.

We were seated in the third row when President Reagan addressed the convention. What a thrill to see him in person. Prayer for him flowed effortlessly from my spirit the whole time he was in our presence. We met a list of national religious leaders and congressmen. I attended a Congressional Breakfast, was furnished with a $25 ticket to an FCC luncheon, and we were presented with two $35 tickets to the culminating banquet.

Our plans were to proceed to Christian Broadcasting Network in Virginia Beach on the way home if the means were available. We were thrilled when we were handed a check the day before we left Washington that would make this side trip possible. As we approached the beach in Virginia, I mentioned to John that it would be super if we could spend the night in a motel on the ocean. The ocean is my favorite place to be, and I had not seen it for a couple years, however, financially it would have been cutting it close, so we decided to head back to Kentucky that afternoon.

When we arrived at CBN one of John's friends took us to lunch, followed by a special "behind the scenes" tour of the facilities. He then announced that he had made arrangements for us to spend the night in an oceanfront motel, and he had taken care of the expenses.

A month later John received a phone call from a couple in our church, who were planning on attending a couple's retreat at Kings Island. Their room and meals were already paid for, but due to some last minute circumstances they were not able to go. They hoped that we could go in their place, all expenses paid. It turned out to be a good quiet weekend—just when we needed it.

That summer the Lord provided the best vacation ever. John was invited to speak at a Full Gospel Businessmen's Dinner in Kill Devil Hills, NC (on the Outer Banks). The men would pay for the gas. John had been helping a puppet ministry in the area, through which we were offered an invitation to stay in a cottage that was two blocks from the ocean.

A month before our vacation our accountant went over our income tax records for the previous three years, and found that some adjusting needed to be done. The government owed us $1300! I was certain this check would come in time to buy some preparations for the trip, pay our children's school registration fees, and give us some breathing room.

As the days drew near our departure date my anxiety dilated into full-blown aggravation. I watched the mailbox like a hawk. Nothing. Thankfully, a young couple from our church gave us a check and earmarked it for our vacation. That check is what got us to the ocean with $40 in our punctured pockets.

We had been obedient in going, trusting that He would provide as He always has, but I drug my chin into Kill Devil Hills murmuring and complaining. The cottage turned out to be a lovely three-bedroom home. We were warmly welcomed with a kitchen counter stacked with food provided by a local Bible study group, with a watermelon and a $20 bill included.

The following afternoon I was standing with the ocean encompassing me to my waist, when a brutal wave literally knocked me off my feet. I had a choice; get out and sit on the sand; stand steeled for the next one and go under again; or relax and ride out the wave. The Lord spoke to my spirit. "Don't try to stand against the rough waves of life. Relax in Me, and I will lift you above them."

On Monday afternoon we called the office. The IRS check had arrived and was being deposited in our account. We had a precious, relaxing time with our three children, completely *care-free.* That is the way it should be all the time. "Casting all your care upon Him; for He cares for you" (1 Peter 5:7).

Jesus said, "Come to Me all you who are heavy laden, and I will give you rest. Take My yoke upon you, and learn from Me; for I am gentle and lowly in heart, and you will find rest for your souls. For My yoke is easy, and My burden is light." (Matthew 11:28-30).

Before we returned home we received another large personal check, which among other things provided for our children to return to school with all the new clothes they needed and wanted (including shoes and extras). My friend also knew that I had been admiring women's suits for three years. A beautiful wool suit was soon hanging in my closet, as well as three new pairs of shoes for the fall.

We stepped out in obedience to God's calling, and He has never failed us. All five of us remained healthy, beautifully clothed, abundantly fed, with every bill paid, and every need met, while we never charged for anything nor took out loans.

The Lord had directed us to enroll our children in a private Christian school in 1981. There was no way in the natural scheme of things that we could afford this. We knew people with high salaries who could not manage to send their children to private school. But God said, "Do it" and we did it. Because of His provision we never missed our monthly tuition payment. We were late a couple of times, but we never missed one.

There was an occasion when we needed almost $500 by a particular Saturday. On Thursday we did not have a penny. $195 was needed to pay our personal and corporate income tax. Almost $300 was needed to pay our phone bill. Southern Bell was going to turn if off on Saturday if the bill was not paid. We did not always receive money in the mail, but Friday we received $185. When John questioned the Lord about the remaining $10, the Holy Spirit reminded him that he had intended to write a thank you note to a man who had sent a check for $10, and the check was still sitting on his desk.

On Saturday morning we were abruptly awakened—someone was pounding on our front door. John jumped up and dashed to the door in an effort to find out what was so urgent. This invigorated young man had been out mowing his lawn when the Lord stopped him and told him to get right over to our house, ask for the phone bill, and pay it!

We are all God's instruments of blessing if we allow Him to use us. As we were obedient to minister to other people's needs, He ministered to ours. We rarely let our needs be known to those around us, but God spoke to His children's hearts when it was time to give.

> Through the Lord's mercies we are not consumed,
> Because His compassions fail not,
> They are new every morning,
> *New every morning*
> Great is Your faithfulness.
> (Lamentations 3:22, 23)

Chapter 20

GOD HAS A PLAN

For I know the thoughts and plans I have for you, says the Lord,
thoughts and plans for welfare and peace and not for evil, to
give you hope in your final outcome.

Jeremiah 29:11 (Amplified)

Jesus is all we need. He's given us each other, health, food, shelter, clothing and most important of all, Himself. A lot of persecution came with this chapter of our lives. People did not understand what we were doing. They thought we were lazy because we did not have regular jobs, but that's okay. God knew we were being obedient, and He was sanding down some rough edges so that some day we will shine like diamonds for Him.

Looking back, the 80s were adventurous years in learning life's lessons. Obedience took on a little different slant for me. For one thing, the Lord led me to write, which opened the door to speaking invitations and leading marriage seminars. I became active as the Prayer Leader for the local Christian Women's Club and the District Representative for Concerned Women for America. Home-schooling our three children, leading discipleship training groups and Evangelism Explosion training kept me growing for three of those years—constant challenges to step out and learn more about myself, God, and the world we live in.

Producing a weekly radio program (For Your Information) kept me busy along with serving on a Christian school board,

111

which provided a segue way into a three year teaching position (the stipend for which went toward Kimberly's college education and my masters in counseling degree program). During the final years of that decade my calling centered on counseling and premarital seminars, but to me the most important lessons were in relationship with my mother. The Lord was not quite done with the healing process between us.

One of my early assignments when working on my counseling degree was to create a genogram, which is basically a family history flow chart. It was an intriguing exercise in itemizing significant details in each one's life and sometimes discovering generational sins that were unknowingly passed from one generation to another. The thing that struck me the hardest was the listing of the traumatic experiences in my mother's life.

Her twin had died at birth. She was left for weeks at a time at an orphanage because her parents did not have food to feed her. She was treated as a slave in her home, and sexually abused by her oldest brother as a young girl. Her father was an alcoholic. She married my father within weeks of their meeting, and after a week's honeymoon he was shipped overseas for two years. She went to live with his parents in another state, where she was treated like trash by my grandmother.

When my father returned from the war she became pregnant with me, but later gave birth to my brother, who lived only a couple days, and later to a stillborn child, followed by several miscarriages caused by an Rh-negative blood condition.

As I studied this list my heart sank for this young woman, and tears of compassion began stream down my face. I felt some of her grief, her despair, and her disappointment. No wonder she acted like an emotional basket case most of the time. No wonder she felt so inferior, so unworthy.

Everything within me wanted to reach out and hold her, and release the love of Jesus to her. Since she lived several states away at this time, I simply picked up the phone and ordered a bouquet of flowers for her, and had the florist sign the card, "Just Because I Love You." There was something powerfully healed in me when I got this glimpse of what my mother's early life had been like. Somehow it enabled me to release a love for her that prevented any visage of offense or hurt from her to ever find a place in my heart again.

The following July a sudden urge to visit my parents gripped my heart. It was a very spur of the moment thing. I had never in my twenty-five years of marriage been homesick for my mom. This was the first time ever that I had made the trip home alone. It turned out to be a low-key, pleasant time of shopping, eating out, and playing cards. Nothing seemed out of the ordinary.

For Christmas that year, I worked overtime to make it a Norman Rockwell memory because our son had received orders saying that he would be headed for the Gulf War in the early months of the New Year. I remember standing in line at the grocery store, embarrassed about spending $50 on ingredients for gingerbread houses. We had never made them as a family before, and had no idea how much fun it would be. It turned out to be well worth the financial investment. Every once in a while I would glance up at mom as we iced and candied our houses—she was as delighted as any little child would be over her very own creation (a small church).

Her eyes twinkled as she watched Daddy, John, and I, along with our two oldest children (in their twenties) playing hide-and-seek in that huge Christian Ministries building—running, squealing with glee, and finding each other in the most unlikely places. Then on Christmas afternoon we played another barrage of original games that kept us laughing until we literally cried. It was the first time that I had ever heard her express how much *fun* she was having.

As Mom and Dad pulled out of the parking lot on a frosty cold January morning, the thought went through my mind that I would never see her again. The weeks passed. In February she called me on a Saturday afternoon just to talk. She had a case of bronchitis and had been to the doctor that morning. She was a little groggy from the medication he had given her, and we laughed about how that was not too unusual for her. I told her I loved her and hung up.

The next morning we received a phone call from Florida saying that my Mom had died in her sleep. How eternally grateful I am that God in His infinite wisdom and grace allowed me to have a joyously healed relationship with my mother before she went to be with Him. Years earlier He had given me the privilege of leading her to receive Him as her personal Savior, so there was absolutely no doubt where she went when she died. She was with Jesus. God sustained me, and empowered me in His overflowing love to preach at her funeral with great joy and thanksgiving for her life. God had a plan.

*   *   *   *   *

"Serving Together" was the logo for Christian Ministries, Inc. John's vision was to be a bridge between various Christian groups and minister to those who were ministering. He served as president of CMI for ten years. During this time he worked with over 250 different missions or ministries.

As the rooms were renovated in the old building by a volunteer staff, offices were provided for various types of ministries rent-free. His vision included providing help for young fledging ministries as well as those that needed a hand up to succeed in terms of administrative assistance, counseling, secretarial services, printing services, mailings, bookkeeping services, computer services, audio and video tape duplication, legal assistance—all staffed by volunteers.

He worked with missionaries, evangelists, children's ministries, musicians, counselors, speakers, writers, teachers, prison ministries, campus ministries, churches of various denominations and other helping ministries. CMI saved these ministries thousands of dollars a year. He ran a thrift store for the poor, helped provide Haitians with medical supplies, and served on the boards of thirty-one ministries.

The Herald Leader reported in their February 5, 1986 issue that Christian Ministries, "a fundamentalist clearinghouse" distributed over one million pieces of Christian literature around the world in the previous year. Little did John know when he began CMI to what extent God was going to use it to further the Gospel. God had a plan.

*   *   *   *   *

Man is a fragile being.

"Just a moment, now," you say, 'We are going to such-and-such a city today or tomorrow. We shall stay there a year doing business and make a profit!' How do you know what will happen even tomorrow? What, after all, is your life? It is like a puff of smoke visible for a little while and then dissolving into thin air. Your remarks should be prefaced with, "If it is the Lord's will, we shall still be alive and will do such-and-such.' As it is, you get a certain pride in yourself in planning your future with such confidence. That sort of pride is all wrong" (James 4:14-16, Phillips).

This kind of pride has resulted in a religion called *humanism,* which is a way of life that blatantly leaves God out, or at best confines Him to a Sunday morning church service, and maybe a meal-time prayer.

For years the Lord has been gently delivering us from Madison Avenue's humanistic brainwashing as to what happiness and success are supposed to look like. Television, radio, magazines, books, music—all kinds of media messengers are used to deceptively dictate a materialistic fantasy world that has no room for God. These feeble counterfeits for reality have eroded our quality of life. As a society we are now comparing our lifestyles to these hollow standards instead of the life-producing standards of God, which He has given us in the Bible.

It is interesting that if we are having a problem with any number of our modern conveniences we take them to an expert to be repaired, or we at least consult the manufacturer's handbook. But when we are experiencing problems in living, we ignore The Expert, and never dream of consulting His powerful Manufacturer's Handbook! How can we deny that The One who made us is The One who knows how we operate best.

I do not expect that Jesus will call you to a lifestyle that He called us to, but He will teach you a whole new way of living right where you are. It will be a real world, an intimate world of knowing Him, loving Him, trusting Him, and learning life lessons that will draw you closer to Him.

Do you desire the reality of Jesus Christ in your life? God has a plan. You can find that reality by yielding to His Spirit right where you are at this moment. Invite Jesus to have His way in your life. Simply pray, "Jesus, I know I have been leaving you out of my life. I have been calling all the shots, and I want You to change me. I ask for Your forgiveness and invite You to take complete control of my life, baptize me afresh in Your Holy Spirit, and teach me Your ways. Amen."

EPILOGUE

While it is my intention to one day write about God's awesome activity in our lives during the 1990s, I do not wish to leave the reader completely adrift concerning what happened to Christian Ministries until then.

On one October afternoon John received a phone call from a young man who was in charge of running the video department for a major missions organization. This young man proceeded to tell him of their desperate need for help. John thoughtfully passed on some names of people he knew who had the skills that would be helpful. When he hung up the phone he felt the Lord was speaking to his spirit, "Why didn't you tell him about you?"

John ran up the stairs and blurted out, "What would you think about going on the mission field?" I had acquired a heart for missions on the day I met Jesus. "Of course I'd be interested." John immediately made plans for us to travel to their international headquarters to meet with the director and get a closer look at the overall mission.

We definitely felt a bond with the director and the vision of the team. We were excited about this new opportunity to serve the Lord. The more we prayed about it, the more this move seemed to be a fit for us. John was going to be the director of operations and I was going to do some work with the women and write for the mission publications. The only hold up was that they required us to raise our support—as in getting people to pledge to send a specified amount of money every month. That felt very uncomfortable to us. We were used to trusting the Lord—not what we felt was going to be pigeonholing people into supporting us. But if this were the route that the Lord wanted us to take we would have to comply with their rules.

To our surprise, when we returned to Lexington we found a friend waiting for us in our carport. Mike Lopez did not know where we had gone or why, but he was waiting for us to ask if we would let him take over Christian Ministries! This really seemed like a direct confirmation from God that we were headed in the right direction. At that time CMI was $4000 in debt. Mike agreed to take care of that debt, but he was going to be moving CMI to the Washington DC area, where he was being transferred.

We spent a year raising our support and moved in November of 1991 for a short stint with the mission organization. CMI flourished in the DC area for a few years, but eventually Mike was transferred to Germany and the ministry dissolved.

"To everything there is a season, and a time for every matter or purpose under heaven" (Ecclesiastes 3:1). There are seasons of seed planting, seasons of growing, seasons of pruning, seasons of harvest, and seasons of dying. Christian Ministries had finished its cycle of seasons. God was moving everyone on in His perfect timing. My "decade of jubilee" was to begin in just a few short years, and I would no longer be a desperate housewife, but forever desperate for more of God!